SANTA FE
TRAVEL GUIDE
2025

GINA T. WATSON

Copyright © 2024 by Gina T. Watson

All rights reserved. No part of this book may be reproduced, distributed, or transmitted in any form or by any means, including photocopying, recording, or other electronic or mechanical methods, without the prior written permission of the publisher, except in the case of brief quotations embodied in critical reviews and specific other noncommercial uses permitted by copyright law

TABLE OF CONTENTS

INTRODUCTION...**6**
   A Brief History and Cultural Heritage................................9
   The Unique Allure of the City Different............................11
   Why Visit Santa Fe..13

CHAPTER 1.
PLANNING YOUR TRIP..**16**
   When to visit Santa Fe..16
   Duration of your trip...19
   Santa Fe on a budget...22
   Choosing the right tour package.......................................25
   Entry and visa requirements...28
   Navigating the City..31

CHAPTER 2.
GETTING TO SANTA FE..**34**
   Choosing the Best flights...34
   Santa Fe airport: Arrival and Orientation........................38
   Journey to Santa Fe...40
   Train Options...42
   Bus Options..44

CHAPTER 3.
WHERE TO STAY IN SANTA FE............................**46**
   Luxury Resorts and Boutique Hotels................................46
   Charming Bed and Breakfasts..49
   Budget-Friendly Accommodations...................................52
   Unique Stays: Adobe Homes and Historic Inns.................56

CHAPTER 4.
SANTA FE'S VIBRANT NEIGHBORHOODS............ 59
- Historic Downtown and the Plaza...................................... 59
- Canyon Road: The Art District... 62
- Railyard and Guadalupe Districts....................................... 65
- Tesuque Village and Surrounding Areas........................... 68

CHAPTER 5.
CULTURAL EXPERIENCES.. 71
- Art Galleries and Studios.. 71
- Museums to Explore... 74
- The Santa Fe Opera: A Summer Spectacle....................... 77
- Traditional Native American Markets.............................. 80
- Santa Fe Events and Festivals.. 82

CHAPTER 6.
LANDMARKS AND ATTRACTIONS....................... 87
- The Historic Santa Fe Plaza.. 87
- Loretto Chapel and the Miraculous Staircase.................. 90
- The Cathedral Basilica of St. Francis of Assisi................. 93
- Meow Wolf: An Immersive Art Adventure....................... 96
- The New Mexico State Capitol... 99

CHAPTER 7.
OUTDOOR ADVENTURES...................................... 102
- Hiking Trails... 102
- Ski Santa Fe: Winter Sports and Year-Round Views...... 106
- Rafting and Water Activities along the Rio Grande........ 109
- Exploring Bandelier National Monument and Kasha-Katuwe Tent Rocks... 112

CHAPTER 8.
FOOD AND DRINK..116
    The Flavors of New Mexican Cuisine.............................. 116
    Iconic Restaurants and Local Favorites.......................... 119
    Farmers' Markets and Food Festivals..........................124
    Breweries, Wineries, and Distilleries.............................. 127

CHAPTER 9.
DAY TRIP AND EXCURSION............................... 130
    Taos and the High Road to Taos......................................130
    Chimayo: A Spiritual and Artistic Getaway..................... 133
    Los Alamos and the Bradbury Science Museum............. 136
    Pecos National Historical Park....................................... 139

CHAPTER 10.
PRACTICAL INFORMATION..................................142
    Safety and Health Considerations..................................142
    Local Etiquette and Cultural Sensitivity.......................... 147
    Money matters and Currency Exchange.........................150
    Language and Communication....................................... 153
    Emergency Contacts... 156
    Useful Websites and Apps... 161
CONCLUSION...164
    MAP.. 167

INTRODUCTION

Santa Fe is a city like no other, a place where the scent of piñon wood mingles with the crisp desert air and where adobe walls seem to glow golden under an endless blue sky. At the foot of the Sangre de Cristo Mountains, this historic capital of New Mexico is a kaleidoscope of natural beauty, cultural vibrancy, and deep-rooted traditions. It's a city that whispers stories of ancient pueblos and Spanish settlers while embracing the creative pulse of modern artists and adventurers. Santa Fe isn't just a destination—it's an invitation to slow down, look closer, and discover something extraordinary.

My own journey to Santa Fe began as a quest for inspiration. I had heard the city's nickname, "The City Different," and I wondered what made it so. Was it the stunning landscapes, the art scene, or the fusion of cultures? My expectations were open-ended, but what I found went far beyond anything I could have imagined. It started with a detour—an unplanned stop on a road trip—because I was drawn to its name on a map. That impulsive decision led me to an entirely new world.

Arriving in Santa Fe was like stepping into a painting. The sun was just setting as I drove into town, and the way the light played off the adobe buildings was nothing short of magical. The streets were alive with music drifting from open doorways, and the aroma of roasted chiles made my stomach rumble in anticipation. My first stop was the Santa Fe Plaza, where I sat on a bench, watching the evening unfold around me. There was a warmth here, not just from the weather but from the people, who seemed genuinely delighted to share their city with anyone willing to explore it.

Over the next few days, Santa Fe revealed itself in layers. I wandered through the Georgia O'Keeffe Museum, where I felt the artist's reverence for the landscape in every brushstroke. I found myself mesmerized by the intricate weavings at the Palace of the Governors, each piece telling a story of heritage and craftsmanship. I stumbled upon a hidden gem of a café in a quiet courtyard, where the sopapillas were fluffy enough to rival the clouds drifting lazily above. And I spent a morning hiking at Bandelier National Monument, marveling at the ancient cliff dwellings carved into the rock, a humbling reminder of those who came long before.

What struck me most was the feeling that Santa Fe isn't a place you simply visit—it's a place that stays with you. Whether it was the earthy smell of rain on desert soil, the meditative silence of the surrounding wilderness, or the lively conversations with locals who spoke of their city with pride, I felt deeply connected to it all. Santa Fe inspired reflection, joy, and a sense of wonder that I carried long after I left.

This guide is my way of sharing that magic with you. It's not just a list of places to see or things to do; it's an invitation to immerse yourself in the heart of Santa Fe. Through these pages, I'll take you beyond the surface, uncovering local secrets, offering practical tips, and painting a vivid picture of what makes this city so special. Whether you're planning your first visit or dreaming of returning, this guide is here to inspire your journey.

So, let's begin. Pack your curiosity, your sense of adventure, and your appetite for discovery. Santa Fe is waiting to enchant you, just as it did me. And who knows? Maybe you'll find something here that changes the way you see the world—or yourself.

A Brief History and Cultural Heritage

Santa Fe has a history as deep and colorful as the desert landscapes that surround it. It's a city that holds stories going back thousands of years, and walking its streets feels like stepping into a living chronicle of human existence. It's one of those places where history is not confined to museums—it's alive in the adobe walls, the markets, and even in the food.

Long before Spanish settlers arrived, the region was home to the Pueblo people, who built thriving communities here as early as 1000 CE. Their connection to the land is evident in everything, from the intricate pottery designs you'll see in local markets to the traditional dances still performed in pueblos around Santa Fe. This ancient culture is the foundation of the city's spirit, and its influence can be seen and felt everywhere you go.

In 1610, the Spanish established Santa Fe as a colonial capital, making it the oldest state capital in the United States. They named it La Villa Real de la Santa Fe de San Francisco de Asís, meaning "The Royal City of the Holy Faith of Saint Francis of Assisi." The Spanish influence is undeniable in the city's architecture, with the adobe buildings, shaded courtyards, and grand churches like the Cathedral Basilica of St. Francis of Assisi. The blending of Spanish and Native American traditions created something entirely unique—what is now celebrated as New Mexican culture.

Over the centuries, Santa Fe became a crossroads for explorers, traders, and settlers. The Santa Fe Trail, a major trade route that connected Missouri to New Mexico, brought waves of people and goods, shaping the city into a bustling trading hub. The mixing of cultures only grew stronger as the Mexican and later American periods added new layers to the city's identity.

Today, Santa Fe is a vibrant showcase of its history and cultural heritage. The city honors its Native American roots with annual events like the Indian Market, where artisans sell handcrafted jewelry, pottery, and textiles. The Spanish influence is celebrated with festivals like the Santa Fe Fiesta, a centuries-old tradition that fills the city with music, food, and parades. Even the city's art scene carries the echoes of its heritage, with works that reflect the natural beauty and cultural depth of the region.

As you explore Santa Fe, you'll see how the past and present come together in perfect harmony. It's in the ancient pueblos that welcome visitors with stories passed down through generations. It's in the historical sites like the Palace of the Governors, where you can still feel the presence of those who came before. It's in the local crafts, the traditional dances, and even in the fiery green chile that defines Santa Fe's cuisine.

Santa Fe isn't just a place to visit; it's a place to experience. Its history is not just about dates and events—it's about the people who lived here, who continue to shape it, and who invite you to be part of their story. Walking through Santa Fe feels like a journey through time, one that you won't forget anytime soon.

The Unique Allure of the City Different

Santa Fe, often called "The City Different," lives up to its nickname in ways that make it truly unforgettable. From the moment you arrive, you sense that this city is unlike anywhere else. It has a character and charm that are hard to define but easy to feel. Nestled in the foothills of the Sangre de Cristo Mountains, Santa Fe's beauty isn't just in its surroundings—it's in its spirit, its people, and its way of life.

The first thing you notice is the architecture. Santa Fe's signature adobe buildings are like works of art in themselves, with soft, earthy tones that blend perfectly with the high desert landscape. The city has strict building codes to preserve this traditional style, so whether you're walking through the historic Plaza or venturing into a quiet neighborhood, you'll see the same harmonious design. It's not just beautiful; it's deeply connected to the city's Native American and Spanish heritage, a reminder of the cultures that built this place.

The art scene here is legendary. Santa Fe has more galleries and museums than you might expect for a city of its size, but that's part of what makes it so special. Canyon Road, a winding street lined with galleries, feels like an open-air museum where you can find everything from contemporary sculptures to traditional Native American pottery. The Georgia O'Keeffe Museum is a must-see, showcasing the work of an artist who captured the essence of New Mexico's landscapes with her bold, vibrant paintings. Art isn't just something you see here—it's something you feel, and it's woven into the everyday life of the city.

Santa Fe is also a place where food becomes an experience. The local cuisine, a blend of Native American, Spanish, and Mexican influences, is as unique as the city itself. The flavors are bold and unforgettable, with green and red chile taking center stage. Whether you're savoring a plate of enchiladas at a local café or treating yourself to a fine dining experience, every bite tells a story. Don't miss the chance to try a green chile cheeseburger or a steaming bowl of posole, especially on a chilly evening.

The city's allure doesn't end in its urban spaces. Just a short drive from the center, the natural beauty of Santa Fe unfolds in every direction. The mountains offer hiking trails with sweeping views, while the desert reveals its quiet magic in every sunrise and sunset. The nearby hot springs and ski slopes add even more to the city's appeal, making it a destination that changes with the seasons.

What truly sets Santa Fe apart is its soul. The city has a way of drawing people in, not just as visitors but as participants in its story. The pace of life here is unhurried, giving you time to connect—with the land, with the people, and with yourself. There's a warmth in the way strangers greet each other, a sense of community that makes you feel like you belong.

Santa Fe is more than just a place to visit; it's a place to experience, to savor, and to remember. It's a city that invites you to slow down, look around, and take it all in. Every moment here feels like a discovery, every corner a chance to see something beautiful. It's a city that stays with you long after you leave, a place that truly lives up to its name as The City Different.

Why Visit Santa Fe

Santa Fe, New Mexico, is a place where history, art, and nature come together to create an experience unlike any other. Known as "The City Different," it beckons travelers with its unique blend of cultures, stunning landscapes, and an atmosphere that feels both timeless and vibrant. Every moment in Santa Fe reveals something special, whether it's the adobe architecture, the vibrant art scene, or the mouthwatering flavors of its cuisine.

One of Santa Fe's most distinctive features is its adobe architecture. Walking through the city feels like stepping into a living canvas of history and culture. The soft, earthy tones of the buildings blend harmoniously with the surrounding desert landscape, creating a visual charm that feels completely unique. The city's Pueblo-Spanish style not only honors its Native American and colonial heritage but also creates a sense of unity and beauty in every corner.

The heart of Santa Fe is its historic Plaza, a lively hub that has been the city's center since the 1600s. It's a place where you can explore the Palace of the Governors, the oldest public building in the United States, and discover the craftsmanship of Native American artisans who display their jewelry and pottery beneath its portal. Nearby, the Loretto Chapel captivates visitors with its mysterious "Miraculous Staircase," a spiral structure that defies architectural logic. For art lovers, the Georgia O'Keeffe Museum showcases the work of an artist whose bold interpretations of the New Mexican landscape have become iconic.

Santa Fe's cultural experiences are as rich as its history. The city comes alive with festivals like the Santa Fe Indian Market, where Native American artists and performers share their heritage with pride, or the International Folk Art Market, which brings together crafts from around the globe. The annual Zozobra festival is a quirky tradition where a massive puppet is burned to symbolize the letting go of worries. Each of these events immerses visitors in the local culture and showcases the vibrant spirit of the community.

The natural beauty of Santa Fe is just as compelling as its cultural offerings. The surrounding Sangre de Cristo Mountains are a haven for outdoor enthusiasts, offering trails that lead to panoramic vistas and serene forests. Ski Santa Fe provides winter sports opportunities, while the Santa Fe Botanical Garden invites visitors to explore the region's unique flora. For those seeking tranquility, the sunsets over the desert are nothing short of magical, painting the sky in hues of orange, pink, and purple.

No visit to Santa Fe is complete without indulging in its culinary delights. The food here is a celebration of bold flavors, with green and red chile taking center stage. Local favorites like green chile stew, enchiladas, and sopapillas offer a taste of the region's heritage. Restaurants like The Shed, known for its traditional New Mexican dishes, and the Santa Fe Farmers Market, where you can sample fresh local produce, provide unforgettable dining experiences.

Many travelers describe Santa Fe as a place that feels alive with creativity and tradition. One visitor shared, "I came for the art, but I stayed for the sunsets and the people. Santa Fe has a way of making you feel like you've found something rare." Another spoke of the city's peaceful charm, saying, "It's a place where the past feels present, and every moment feels meaningful."

Planning a trip to Santa Fe is easy, with its accessibility from major cities and a welcoming vibe for all types of travelers. The best time to visit is during the spring or fall when the weather is mild, and the city's events are in full swing. Families will enjoy the interactive exhibits at the Santa Fe Children's Museum, couples can find romance in the city's cozy inns, and solo travelers will discover endless inspiration in the art and landscapes.

Santa Fe isn't just a destination—it's an experience that stays with you. Its mix of history, culture, and natural beauty creates a tapestry that's both fascinating and deeply personal. Whether you're seeking adventure, relaxation, or a deeper connection to the world, Santa Fe has something to offer. Step into The City Different and discover a place that will capture your heart and leave you longing to return.

CHAPTER 1.
PLANNING YOUR TRIP
When to visit Santa Fe

Santa Fe is a destination that offers something magical in every season, transforming its landscape and atmosphere to suit different kinds of travelers. Each season brings its own charm, from blooming gardens in the spring to the snow-dusted adobe walls of winter. Knowing what to expect throughout the year can help you tailor your visit to your preferences and interests.

Spring in Santa Fe feels like a gentle awakening, as the city emerges from the chill of winter with mild temperatures and a burst of natural beauty. The high desert landscape becomes alive with wildflowers, and the crisp air is perfect for exploring the outdoors. Days are comfortably warm, with temperatures ranging from the high 50s to mid-70s, while evenings can be cool, so a light jacket is essential. This is also a wonderful time to visit the Santa Fe Botanical Garden, where native plants like chamisa and yucca begin to bloom, creating a serene oasis against the rugged desert backdrop.

Spring is also the season of renewal, and the city's art scene reflects this with events like the Santa Fe Studio Tour, where visitors can meet local artists in their creative spaces. Hiking trails, such as those in the nearby Pecos Wilderness or along the Dale Ball Trails, are less crowded and showcase the region's lush transformation. Spring tends to be quieter than summer, meaning lower accommodation rates and a more relaxed atmosphere for exploring the city's galleries and museums.

Summer in Santa Fe is vibrant and alive, a season of energy and celebration. The warm days and cooler evenings invite visitors to enjoy outdoor events, from the Santa Fe Opera's breathtaking open-air performances to the famed Santa Fe Indian Market in August, a gathering of Native American artists and craftspeople that showcases the city's deep cultural roots. Temperatures can range from the mid-80s during the day to a refreshing 50s at night, making it essential to pack layers, sunscreen, and a wide-brimmed hat to protect against the strong desert sun.

Summer also brings opportunities to enjoy Santa Fe's natural beauty. Outdoor enthusiasts will relish the chance to explore Bandelier National Monument or take a scenic drive up to Hyde Memorial State Park, where higher elevations provide a cool escape. Farmers' markets buzz with fresh produce, and the city's outdoor patios are ideal for dining under the stars. However, summer is also peak tourist season, so it's wise to book accommodations and event tickets in advance to secure the best options.

Autumn in Santa Fe is a time of golden light and crisp air, when the city's charm takes on a quieter, more reflective tone. The aspens in the Sangre de Cristo Mountains turn brilliant shades of gold, and the smell of roasting green chile wafts through the streets, marking the start of chile harvest season. Daytime temperatures in the 60s and 70s, coupled with cooler nights, create an ideal climate for outdoor adventures and leisurely strolls through the historic Plaza.

One of the highlights of fall is the Albuquerque International Balloon Fiesta, located just an hour's drive away. This spectacular event fills the skies with vibrant hot-air balloons, and Santa Fe serves as a serene base for exploring the festivities. The city also celebrates its culinary traditions with the Santa Fe Wine and Chile Fiesta, a perfect opportunity to savor local flavors and pair them with regional wines. Autumn tends to be less crowded than summer, making it an excellent time to explore the city's museums, such as the New Mexico History Museum or the Museum of International Folk Art, without the peak-season bustle.

Winter in Santa Fe is pure enchantment, as the city transforms into a winter wonderland with its snow-covered adobe buildings and cozy atmosphere. Temperatures range from the high 40s during the day to chilly evenings in the teens, so warm clothing, gloves, and sturdy footwear are essential. This is a season for both relaxation and celebration, as the city comes alive with holiday traditions. Farolito-lined streets during Christmas Eve create a magical scene, and the glow of the luminarias along Canyon Road adds a festive warmth to the crisp winter air.

Winter is also perfect for outdoor activities, with Ski Santa Fe offering powdery slopes just a short drive from the city. After a day of adventure, soaking in the natural mineral waters at Ojo Caliente or indulging in a hot chocolate at one of Santa Fe's charming cafes is the perfect way to unwind. Crowds are thinner than in summer, and this off-season period often brings discounted rates on accommodations, making it an attractive time for budget-conscious travelers.

Choosing the best time to visit Santa Fe depends on your personal interests. Spring and fall offer mild weather and fewer crowds, making them ideal for leisurely exploration and outdoor activities. Summer brims with cultural energy and events, while winter provides a peaceful retreat with the added bonus of festive charm. Each season has its own distinct allure, ensuring that Santa Fe remains captivating no matter when you choose to visit.

Duration of your trip

Planning the duration of your trip to Santa Fe depends on what you hope to experience in this enchanting city. Santa Fe is rich in culture, history, art, and natural beauty, and there's so much to explore, whether you're visiting for a weekend, a week, or even longer. Let's take a closer look at how much time you might want to dedicate to your trip based on your interests.

For a short weekend getaway, two to three days can give you a taste of Santa Fe's vibrant spirit. Start your journey in the heart of the city at the historic Plaza. You can spend your first day strolling through the surrounding streets, visiting landmarks like the Palace of the Governors and the Cathedral Basilica of St. Francis of Assisi. In the evening, savor local flavors with a meal featuring green or red chile at a nearby restaurant. Day two might take you to Canyon Road, where art galleries line the street, showcasing everything from Native

American crafts to contemporary masterpieces. If you have time, a short hike or a visit to one of the nearby pueblos can add a touch of nature or cultural depth to your brief stay.

For a longer visit of four to five days, you can immerse yourself more fully in Santa Fe's offerings. In addition to exploring the Plaza and Canyon Road, dedicate a day to visiting the remarkable museums on Museum Hill, such as the Museum of International Folk Art and the Wheelwright Museum of the American Indian. Reserve another day for outdoor activities, like hiking in the Sangre de Cristo Mountains or exploring the ancient ruins at Bandelier National Monument. Evenings can be spent enjoying live music, opera, or a peaceful stroll through the Railyard Arts District. Don't forget to set aside time to explore Santa Fe's unique shops and markets, where you can find handcrafted jewelry, pottery, and textiles.

A week in Santa Fe allows you to fully experience the city's diverse attractions and nearby treasures. With seven days, you can spread out your activities and explore at a relaxed pace. Consider venturing beyond the city limits to destinations like Taos, known for its historic pueblo and striking Rio Grande Gorge Bridge. Take a scenic drive on the High Road to Taos, stopping at quaint villages and churches along the way. You'll also have time to enjoy some indulgence, such as soaking in the mineral springs at Ojo Caliente or attending a wellness retreat. With a full week, you can participate in workshops, art classes, or cooking lessons, giving you a deeper connection to Santa Fe's artistic and culinary heritage.

If your schedule allows for an extended stay of two weeks or more, Santa Fe becomes your base for an even wider range of adventures. You can dive into the city's festivals and events, such as the Indian Market or the International Folk Art Market, which often require extra time to fully appreciate. Longer trips also mean you can explore the surrounding areas at your leisure, from the Jemez Mountains to the historic Route 66. An extended visit gives you the chance to experience the rhythm of daily life in Santa Fe, enjoying its cafes, parks, and quiet moments that often go unnoticed during shorter trips.

No matter how long you stay, Santa Fe promises to captivate you with its charm and endless discoveries. If you have limited time, focus on the essentials and soak in the city's unique energy. With more time, you can uncover the layers of history, culture, and natural beauty that make Santa Fe a place unlike any other.

Santa Fe on a budget

Exploring Santa Fe on a budget is not only possible but can also enhance your experience as you uncover its authentic charm and enjoy its highlights without stretching your wallet. The city, with its blend of art, history, and natural beauty, offers a wealth of affordable and free experiences, making it an excellent destination for travelers who want to save while still diving into its unique appeal.

Timing your visit can significantly impact your budget. Santa Fe's shoulder seasons, particularly late spring and early fall, are perfect times to visit. During these periods, accommodation prices often drop compared to peak summer months or the winter holiday season. The weather is still delightful, allowing you to enjoy outdoor activities and festivals without the crowds. You'll find better deals and a more relaxed atmosphere, making your trip both economical and enjoyable.

When it comes to accommodation, Santa Fe has plenty of options for budget-conscious travelers. Look into hostels like The Santa Fe International Hostel, which offers affordable dormitory-style rooms and a community atmosphere. Vacation rentals can also be a cost-effective option, especially if you're traveling with a group and can split expenses. Websites like Airbnb and Vrbo often list cozy casitas or apartments at reasonable rates. For those who love the outdoors, consider camping at nearby locations like Hyde Memorial State Park, where you can enjoy the beauty of nature for a fraction of the cost of a hotel.

Planning activities around affordable attractions is another way to keep expenses in check. Many of Santa Fe's cultural landmarks, such as the Plaza and its surrounding historic sites, are free to visit. Spend a day wandering Canyon Road, admiring the art galleries, and enjoying the street's creative energy without needing to make a purchase. Museums like the New Mexico History Museum or the Georgia O'Keeffe Museum often have discounted admission days or free entry during specific times. Keep an eye out for community events, local markets, and festivals, which provide entertainment and a glimpse into the local culture at little to no cost.

Dining on a budget in Santa Fe can be a treat, as the city offers a range of affordable options that let you savor its renowned cuisine. Look for local favorites like Tia Sophia's, known for its hearty breakfast burritos, or The Shed, which serves traditional New Mexican dishes at reasonable prices. Food trucks and casual eateries like El Chile Toreado are excellent choices for enjoying flavorful meals without breaking the bank. For an even more budget-friendly option, shop at the Santa Fe Farmers' Market and create your picnic with fresh, local produce. Many parks and scenic spots around the city provide perfect settings for a relaxed, inexpensive meal.

Getting around Santa Fe can be affordable with careful planning. The city is compact, and many attractions are within walking distance of each other, especially in the downtown area. For longer distances, public transportation like the Santa Fe Trails bus system is a budget-friendly option. If you're planning to explore the surrounding area, consider renting a bike or taking advantage of shared rides to split costs. Some museums and attractions offer combo tickets or passes that provide access to multiple sites at a discounted rate.

To make the most of your budget-friendly trip, research discounts and special offers ahead of time. Many local attractions and restaurants have promotions for visitors, and staying flexible with your plans can help you take advantage of last-minute deals. Santa Fe's charm lies in its authenticity, and often, the best experiences—like watching a breathtaking sunset over the desert or strolling through a quiet pueblo—are entirely free.

Even on a modest budget, Santa Fe offers unforgettable experiences that highlight its culture, history, and natural beauty. By timing your visit wisely, seeking out affordable accommodations, and focusing on free or low-cost activities, you can immerse yourself in the city's magic without spending lavishly. This approach ensures a rich and fulfilling trip, proving that the most meaningful adventures don't have to come with a high price tag.

Choosing the right tour package

Selecting the best tour packages for Santa Fe is a crucial step in making your visit as enjoyable and enriching as possible. Santa Fe offers an array of tour options that cater to a wide variety of interests, from art and history enthusiasts to outdoor adventurers. By understanding the different types of tours available, their specific details, and the suitability for different travelers, you can choose a package that fits your preferences and budget.

Santa Fe boasts a range of tour types, each offering a unique way to experience the city and its surroundings. Guided tours are an excellent choice for those who enjoy in-depth narratives and expert insights. These include options like historical walking tours of the Plaza, which typically last two to three hours and cost around $25 to $50 per person. Guides delve into Santa Fe's rich history, taking visitors through landmarks such as the San Miguel Chapel and the Palace of the Governors. For those looking to explore at their own pace, self-guided walking tours are a flexible alternative. Apps and guidebooks provide detailed itineraries for exploring Santa Fe's art districts or historic neighborhoods, often for a minimal fee or free.

Adventure tours offer a chance to immerse yourself in Santa Fe's breathtaking natural surroundings. Hiking excursions in the Sangre de Cristo Mountains or hot air balloon rides over the desert are popular choices. A half-day hiking tour might cost around $75, including transportation and a knowledgeable guide who can share insights about the local flora and fauna. Hot air balloon rides, while pricier at $200 to

$300, provide an unforgettable experience with stunning views of the high desert landscape.

Choosing the right tour depends on your travel group and interests. Families with children may enjoy tours that include interactive elements, such as a family-friendly exploration of the Santa Fe Children's Museum or a pottery-making workshop at a local artist's studio. Couples might find romantic appeal in sunset hiking tours or private wine-tasting excursions that include visits to nearby vineyards. Solo travelers often appreciate the camaraderie of group walking tours or the meditative solitude of a self-guided hike. Groups can benefit from customized packages, such as private cultural tours or food and art experiences tailored to their shared interests.

Seasonal factors can greatly influence the availability and appeal of certain tour packages. Summer and fall are ideal for outdoor adventures like hiking and biking, as the weather is warm and the landscapes are vibrant. Winter tours, such as snowshoeing or exploring Santa Fe's festive holiday markets, offer a completely different perspective. During spring, you might opt for cultural tours that coincide with art events like the Santa Fe Film Festival or outdoor excursions to enjoy blooming wildflowers. Booking seasonal tours in advance is essential, as popular options fill up quickly during peak times.

Local guides and seasoned travelers often recommend less conventional tours that showcase Santa Fe's hidden gems. Ghost tours of the city offer a thrilling exploration of its spookier legends, while culinary tours introduce visitors to hidden eateries and local delicacies. A market tour might include stops at the Santa Fe Farmers' Market and cooking demonstrations with traditional New Mexican ingredients. These niche experiences are often highly rated and provide insights into aspects of Santa Fe that standard tours may overlook.

When booking a tour package, it is wise to research thoroughly. Look for reputable operators with strong reviews, and consider booking directly through local agencies to ensure authenticity and support small businesses. Checking for discounts, such as early bird deals or group rates, can also help save money. Online platforms like Viator and GetYourGuide often list a variety of options, but it's always a good idea to cross-check with the tour operator's official website to confirm details.

For those who prefer flexibility, many tour providers allow for customization. You can mix and match activities, creating a unique itinerary that includes both guided and self-guided experiences. For instance, you could combine a half-day historical tour with an afternoon cooking class, ensuring a day that caters to your specific interests and pace.

Ultimately, the right tour package for you will depend on your travel goals, interests, and the time you have in Santa Fe. By carefully considering your preferences, reading reviews, and planning ahead, you can find a tour that not only meets your needs but enhances your overall experience of this enchanting city. Taking the time to explore the variety of options ensures that your trip to Santa Fe will be as memorable and fulfilling as possible.

Entry and visa requirements

When planning a trip to Santa Fe, understanding the visa and entry requirements is an essential step for international travelers. Santa Fe is located in the United States, so the entry requirements depend largely on your nationality and travel history. While the process can vary slightly, here's a detailed guide to help you navigate through visa requirements, the application process, and offer some practical tips to ensure your trip goes smoothly.

To determine if you need a visa for travel to Santa Fe, the first thing to check is your nationality and the type of passport you hold. Citizens from countries that are part of the U.S. Visa Waiver Program (VWP) do not need a visa for short visits (up to 90 days) for tourism, business, or transit purposes. However, they must apply for an ESTA (Electronic System for Travel Authorization) prior to their travel. If your country is not part of the VWP, then a visa is required to enter the United States. For most travelers, this will be a B-2 tourist visa, but there are other types, such as B-1 for business or F-1 for students, depending on your purpose of visit.

The visa application process for Santa Fe, and the U.S. in general, involves several steps that need to be followed carefully. Start by filling out the DS-160 form, which is the online application form required for most non-immigrant visas. After completing the form, you'll need to pay the application fee. Once the payment is made, you will schedule an appointment at your nearest U.S. embassy or consulate for a visa interview. Keep in mind that visa processing times can vary depending on your country of residence, so it is always recommended to apply well in advance of your planned travel date.

During your visa interview, you will need to present several documents to support your application. The basic requirements typically include a valid passport, a recent passport-sized photo, the confirmation page from the DS-160 form, and proof of payment for the visa application fee. In addition, you may need to provide evidence of your travel plans, including flight reservations, accommodation bookings, and proof of financial means to show that you can support yourself during your stay in the United States. Some applicants may also be asked for additional documents, such as an invitation letter, travel insurance, or proof of ties to your home country, which assures the consulate that you plan to return after your trip.

Practical tips for a smooth visa application process include checking the visa requirements well in advance, as the process can sometimes take several weeks, especially during busy travel seasons. Always rely on official government websites, such as the U.S. Department of State website, for the most up-to-date and accurate information. Double-check all documentation before submitting your application to avoid delays. It's also helpful to gather extra documents to demonstrate the purpose of your trip and your intent to return home, as consular officers may ask for additional information during the interview.

To make the process easier, interactive tools such as online visa checkers or a flowchart can be useful for visualizing each step of the application process. For instance, you can follow a simple flowchart starting from identifying your visa requirement, then completing the DS-160, scheduling your interview, attending the interview with all required documents, and waiting for your visa approval.

Let's look at some example scenarios to help illustrate how the process might differ depending on nationality. For a traveler from the United Kingdom, as part of the VWP, they would not need a visa for a short stay of up to 90 days, but they would still need to apply for ESTA. On the other hand, a traveler from India, who is not part of the VWP, would need to apply for a B-2 tourist visa by following the complete process: filling out the DS-160 form, attending a visa interview, and providing supporting documents such as a letter from their employer and proof of sufficient funds.

In conclusion, while applying for a visa to visit Santa Fe can seem like a complex process, careful preparation and understanding of the requirements can help ensure a smooth and successful application. Always plan ahead, gather all necessary documentation, and rely on trusted official sources for guidance. By following these steps, you'll be well on your way to enjoying your trip to Santa Fe without any unnecessary travel setbacks.

Navigating the City

Navigating Santa Fe is a pleasant experience with various transportation options that allow visitors to explore the city at their own pace. Whether you prefer public transport, walking, or renting a car, there are convenient ways to get around this beautiful and vibrant city.

For those looking to use public transport, Santa Fe offers a reliable bus system. The Santa Fe Trails buses are the primary form of public transport, and they cover various routes throughout the city, making it easy to visit popular spots like the historic Plaza, art galleries, and the Railyard District. The buses are affordable and run regularly, though it's a good idea to check the schedules ahead of time as the service might not be as frequent in the evenings or on weekends. A day pass is available, offering unlimited rides, which is great for those who plan to use the bus several times during their visit. You can pay for your fare with cash or by using a smart card that can be purchased at local convenience stores.

If you enjoy exploring a city on foot, Santa Fe is perfect for walking. The compact size of the city makes it easy to get around on foot, and much of the charm lies in wandering through its narrow streets, admiring its adobe-style architecture, and discovering hidden shops and galleries. Santa Fe's downtown area is particularly walkable, and the Plaza is a great starting point. From there, you can stroll along the historic streets, such as Canyon Road, known for its numerous art galleries, or head toward the peaceful paths of the Santa Fe River Trail for a more nature-filled walk. Many of the city's best attractions are within walking distance of each other, so you can take your time and enjoy the sights without having to rush or worry about transportation.

For those who prefer more flexibility and want to venture beyond the city center, renting a car is a great option. Renting a car allows you to explore not just Santa Fe but also the surrounding landscapes, such as the scenic Sangre de Cristo Mountains or the famous Georgia O'Keeffe Museum in Abiquiú. Car rentals are widely available at the Santa Fe Municipal Airport, as well as in downtown locations. If you're planning to drive, be aware that parking in the downtown area can be limited, especially during busy times, so it's helpful to know where the public parking lots are located or check out the city's free parking options. Driving around Santa Fe is generally straightforward, as the roads are well-marked, and traffic is typically not an issue unless you're visiting during peak tourist seasons.

If you're not familiar with driving in the area, there are also taxi services, ride-sharing options like Uber and Lyft, and even bike rentals. Santa Fe's bike-friendly environment, with bike lanes and paths, makes cycling an enjoyable way to explore, especially in the warmer months. You can find bike rentals downtown, and there are several bike tours available for those who want to learn more about the city's history and culture while cycling.

Each mode of transportation in Santa Fe comes with its own set of advantages, depending on your preferences. If you prefer a relaxed, leisurely visit, walking is ideal, allowing you to soak in the atmosphere at your own pace. For convenience and cost-effectiveness, public transport is an excellent option, especially if you want to visit different neighborhoods without worrying about parking. On the other hand, renting a car gives you the freedom to explore not just the city but the surrounding areas as well, making it a good choice for those who want to venture further.

No matter how you choose to get around, Santa Fe offers a variety of ways to see the sights, each providing a unique experience. Whether you're strolling along its charming streets or driving to a nearby natural wonder, you'll find plenty of ways to navigate the city and make the most of your time there.

CHAPTER 2.

GETTING TO SANTA FE

Choosing the Best flights

When planning a trip to Santa Fe, selecting the right flight is essential to ensure both comfort and cost-effectiveness. The city itself does not have a large international airport, but there are several options for travelers flying in. Major airlines offer routes to Santa Fe and surrounding airports, each with its own set of conveniences and costs. Santa Fe's closest airport is the Santa Fe Municipal Airport (SAF), but travelers also often use the Albuquerque International Sunport (ABQ), which is about an hour's drive away.

Several major airlines, such as American Airlines, Delta, and United, offer flights to Santa Fe, though direct flights to SAF are relatively limited. American Airlines typically operates daily flights from Dallas/Fort Worth International Airport, with a flight duration of around 1 hour and 30 minutes. Other routes, such as from Denver, might require a layover depending on the airline, but the total travel time can range from 3 to 4 hours. United Airlines offers similar routes through larger hubs like Denver and Houston. In general, connecting flights through major cities like Dallas or Denver are more common, with layovers often adding a few hours to the total travel time.

To find the best deals on flights to Santa Fe, it's important to be strategic. Booking well in advance, ideally 2-3 months before your trip, can help secure better prices. Being flexible with your travel dates is also key to finding the lowest fares. Sometimes adjusting your departure or return dates by just a day or two can result in a significant price difference. Using flight comparison websites like Skyscanner, Kayak, or Google Flights allows you to compare prices across multiple airlines and dates, giving you a clear idea of the best deals. Setting fare alerts through these platforms is also a good way to monitor price drops and book when the fare is at its lowest.

Flight prices can vary depending on the season. Peak travel times to Santa Fe are typically during the summer months, from June to August, when the weather is warm, and the city is bustling with tourists. Flight prices during this period tend to be higher due to increased demand. The shoulder seasons, such as spring (March to May) and fall (September to November), offer a good balance of pleasant weather and lower flight costs. Winter, while less popular for traditional tourism, is also a time when you might find great deals, particularly if you're willing to deal with colder weather and a quieter atmosphere. To get the most value for money, consider traveling during the shoulder seasons or winter months, as these tend to be more affordable while still offering a memorable experience in Santa Fe.

When booking flights, it's also important to be aware of any additional airport fees and taxes that might be added to your ticket price. Santa Fe Municipal Airport itself does not have particularly high fees, but taxes can add up. Travelers departing from larger airports like Dallas or Denver may also face additional charges related to security fees, baggage handling, and fuel surcharges. To minimize these costs, always check the total cost of the flight, including any taxes and fees, before booking.

Baggage policies are another factor to consider when selecting a flight. Major airlines like American Airlines, United, and Delta typically include one free carry-on bag in the ticket price, though each airline has specific size and weight restrictions. For checked baggage, expect to pay an additional fee, which can range from $30 to $50 for the first checked bag, depending on the airline and your ticket class. If you have oversized luggage, such as a ski bag or large gear, check the airline's policies for additional fees and weight limits to avoid surprises at the airport. Be sure to review the baggage allowance and fees when booking your flight so that you can pack accordingly and avoid additional charges at check-in.

For travelers who seek more comfort, there are different travel classes available, ranging from economy to first class. Economy class, which is the most affordable option, typically includes basic services such as a seat, entertainment, and snacks. Premium economy offers a bit more space and additional amenities such as priority boarding and extra luggage allowance. Business class provides more comfortable seating, larger personal space, and priority service, making it ideal for those who want a more luxurious experience. First class offers the highest level of comfort, with fully reclining seats, high-end meals, and exclusive service. While these upgrades come at a higher cost, they can be worth it for those seeking a premium experience. It's important to compare the price differences and services offered by each class when booking.

Booking tips for flights to Santa Fe include taking the time to research your options thoroughly. Many airlines offer online booking with various options for travel insurance, baggage add-ons, and flexibility in case you need to change your travel plans. When booking through travel agencies or third-party websites, always check the airline's own site to ensure the most accurate and up-to-date pricing and availability. Cancellation policies vary, so be sure to read the fine print and consider purchasing travel insurance if you're concerned about potential changes to your trip.

Frequent travelers to Santa Fe may benefit from joining airline loyalty programs, which allow you to accumulate miles and earn rewards for future flights. Major airlines like American Airlines, Delta, and United all have loyalty programs that offer perks such as free checked bags, priority boarding, and access to exclusive lounges. Signing up for these programs can provide long-term benefits if you plan to visit Santa Fe regularly or if you travel often in general.

Selecting the best flight to Santa Fe depends on your travel needs, budget, and schedule. By researching flight options, booking in advance, and being flexible with travel dates, you can ensure a cost-effective and comfortable journey. Whether you're flying directly into Santa Fe or using Albuquerque as a hub, planning ahead and considering factors like baggage policies and seasonal variations will help make your trip seamless. With a little research and preparation, you can find the perfect flight that fits both your schedule and your budget.

Santa Fe airport: Arrival and Orientation

Arriving at Santa Fe Municipal Airport (SAF) feels welcoming and convenient, especially for travelers heading to this beautiful city. While it's a smaller airport compared to major hubs, it provides everything you need to get settled and start your trip with ease.

As soon as you step off the plane, you'll notice how quiet and easy-going the airport is. This makes for a relaxed arrival experience. Santa Fe Municipal Airport serves both domestic and regional flights, so most travelers come in from major cities like Dallas or Denver. The airport has a single terminal, which means you won't have to navigate through complex layouts. It's simple and quick to find your way around, and the baggage claim area is just a short walk from where you'll deplane.

After you collect your luggage, you'll be greeted by helpful airport staff who can answer any questions and direct you to the ground transportation options. If you need to rent a car, there are rental agencies right on-site. You'll find cars from major companies like Hertz, Enterprise, and Avis. It's a good idea to reserve your vehicle ahead of time, especially during peak travel seasons, to ensure availability. Rental counters are easy to locate, and the whole process is smooth and quick. If you prefer not to rent a car, you can also find taxis and ride-sharing services like Uber and Lyft, which provide an efficient and affordable way to get to your accommodation.

If you're not in a rush and want to soak in some of Santa Fe's charm right away, you can take advantage of the local shuttle services. Some hotels offer free shuttle rides to and from the airport, so be sure to check with your accommodation in advance if this is an option. The airport is only about 10 minutes from downtown Santa Fe, so whether you're in a taxi, shuttle, or rental car, you won't have a long journey before you're right in the heart of the city.

Inside the airport, the amenities are basic but sufficient for most travelers. You'll find a small café where you can grab a coffee or snack before heading out. There's also free Wi-Fi, so you can easily check in with family or update your travel plans. If you need any last-minute travel essentials or souvenirs, there's a small gift shop where you can pick up local products or a travel guide to help you explore Santa Fe.

Once you leave the airport, the surrounding area is easy to navigate. Santa Fe's downtown area, with its historic adobe architecture and unique art scene, is just a short drive away, making it a perfect starting point for your adventure. Whether you're heading to your hotel, exploring the city, or simply taking in the sights, getting oriented in Santa Fe is a breeze. The welcoming atmosphere at the airport is just the beginning of the warmth you'll experience in this stunning city.

Journey to Santa Fe

The journey to Santa Fe is like stepping into a new world, where the landscape shifts and the rhythm of life slows down. Whether you're arriving by car, bus, or plane, the experience of getting to Santa Fe is a scenic adventure that sets the tone for the magic of this charming city.

For those arriving by car, the journey to Santa Fe can be as memorable as the destination itself. Driving into the city is an invitation to take in the vast landscapes that stretch out in every direction. From Albuquerque, about an hour's drive south, the route offers a chance to experience the wide expanses of New Mexico's desert terrain. The Sandia Mountains in the distance provide a beautiful backdrop as you head north. The road leading to Santa Fe is surrounded by juniper trees and sagebrush, with the occasional small town offering a stop for gas or a bite to eat. The scenic drive gives you a sense of space and peace, with long stretches of road where the only sound is the wind.

If you're coming from the east, the drive through the high plains will introduce you to the beauty of the vast, open sky and the red rock formations that characterize New Mexico's landscape. It's a quiet, meditative route where the land feels alive with history, especially as you approach Santa Fe. The city's unique adobe-style architecture and vibrant cultural scene will soon be visible, welcoming you into one of the most storied cities in America.

Traveling to Santa Fe by bus is another option, with several bus services connecting the city to nearby areas like

Albuquerque and other major New Mexico destinations. The bus ride offers a comfortable and affordable way to experience the landscape, though it may take a little longer than driving yourself. The buses generally offer a scenic route through the desert, with wide windows that allow you to enjoy the views of the surrounding mesas, mountains, and small towns.

The journey to Santa Fe, however you choose to make it, is a special experience. The city is not just a destination, but a place that invites you to slow down and take in the surroundings. As you get closer to the heart of Santa Fe, the warmth of its culture and the richness of its history begin to make themselves known. Whether you've traveled for hours or just arrived from a nearby town, Santa Fe is a place that immediately feels welcoming, like a new home in the desert.

Train Options

Traveling to Santa Fe by train is an experience that offers both comfort and scenic beauty, making it an excellent option for those who want to enjoy the journey as much as the destination. While Santa Fe itself does not have a direct major train station, nearby cities like Albuquerque provide access to Amtrak routes that can connect you to this charming New Mexico city.

The most common way to travel by train to Santa Fe is to take an Amtrak service to Albuquerque, which is about an hour's drive from the city. Albuquerque is well-connected to major cities across the U.S., so depending on where you're coming from, you can enjoy a long-distance scenic journey. Amtrak's Southwest Chief, which runs between Chicago and Los Angeles, is one of the primary routes you might take to get to Albuquerque. This train ride offers a relaxing experience with spacious seating, dining options, and beautiful views of the American landscape, particularly through the Southwest's desert and mountainous regions.

Once you arrive in Albuquerque, you can take a quick bus ride or rent a car to get to Santa Fe. The bus ride between Albuquerque and Santa Fe is direct and takes around 1 to 1.5 hours, providing a seamless way to complete your journey. The bus service is convenient and reasonably priced, making it a great option for travelers on a budget. The ride itself is an extension of the scenic experience, passing through New Mexico's striking landscapes.

For those looking for a bit more adventure, consider taking the New Mexico Rail Runner Express, a commuter train that operates between Albuquerque and Santa Fe. While it's a more local service, it offers an affordable and pleasant way to experience the area. The New Mexico Rail Runner is known for its panoramic windows, giving travelers a chance to enjoy the beautiful scenery of the Rio Grande Valley and the surrounding desert. The train ride is comfortable, with spacious seating and stops in various small towns along the way, making it a relaxing and convenient choice for getting to Santa Fe from Albuquerque.

Train travel is a wonderful way to experience New Mexico's landscapes in a relaxed, stress-free manner. The smooth ride allows you to unwind, while the ever-changing scenery outside your window offers glimpses of the rugged beauty of the Southwest. Even though you'll need to make a transfer in Albuquerque to reach Santa Fe, the journey itself is a delightful way to start your visit to this historic and enchanting city. Whether you're on the Southwest Chief or the New Mexico Rail Runner, taking the train gives you the opportunity to experience the journey in a way that feels as memorable as the destination itself.

Bus Options

Taking a bus to Santa Fe is a convenient and affordable way to reach this beautiful city. While Santa Fe itself doesn't have a large bus station for long-distance services, nearby Albuquerque serves as the main hub for many bus routes. From Albuquerque, it's easy to continue your journey to Santa Fe with several options available.

If you're coming from Albuquerque, the most common and direct way to get to Santa Fe is by using the Greyhound bus service. Greyhound operates regular routes that connect major cities across the U.S. to Albuquerque. Once you arrive in Albuquerque, you can hop on a bus that will take you directly to Santa Fe. The trip from Albuquerque to Santa Fe by bus usually takes about 1 to 1.5 hours, passing through the scenic New Mexican landscape, making the ride comfortable and relaxing.

Another option from Albuquerque to Santa Fe is the New Mexico Park and Ride service, which is a local commuter bus that runs multiple times a day. These buses are clean, well-maintained, and offer a smooth ride. It's a very affordable option and is especially popular for those looking for budget-friendly transportation. The New Mexico Park and Ride buses are well-timed, making it easy to plan your arrival in Santa Fe.

For travelers coming from further away, you can also take a Greyhound bus to Albuquerque from various cities in the region or beyond. Once in Albuquerque, transferring to a local bus or using a rental car to get to Santa Fe is straightforward.

The Greyhound stations in Albuquerque are centrally located and are connected to other local transport options, so it's easy to find your way to your next leg of the journey.

Buses are a practical option for those who want a smooth and budget-friendly journey to Santa Fe. The bus services are generally reliable and offer good amenities like air conditioning and free Wi-Fi on some routes, making your travel more comfortable. It's also an excellent way to meet fellow travelers along the way and enjoy the relaxed pace of the journey.

While buses may take a little longer than other forms of transportation, such as flying or driving, they offer a more affordable and scenic experience. The route from Albuquerque to Santa Fe, in particular, is a pleasant one, with beautiful views of the desert and mountains that you can enjoy from the window. Whether you're looking to save on travel costs or simply prefer the bus as a mode of transportation, this option offers a convenient and comfortable way to explore New Mexico.

CHAPTER 3.
WHERE TO STAY IN SANTA FE

Luxury Resorts and Boutique Hotels

When you step into Santa Fe, you'll find a wealth of places to stay that truly capture the essence of the city. Whether you're looking for a luxury resort with every indulgence or a boutique hotel that feels like a cozy, unique escape, Santa Fe offers a range of accommodations that provide an authentic experience.

The **Four Seasons Resort Rancho** Encantado Santa Fe is one of the most luxurious resorts in the area, nestled on 57 acres of pristine desert landscape. Located at 198 NM-592, this resort is just a short 15-minute drive from downtown Santa Fe. Upon arriving, you're welcomed by a serene atmosphere, with adobe-style architecture that perfectly complements the desert surroundings. The resort offers a range of activities, from relaxing by the stunning outdoor pool to indulging in a spa treatment. The restaurant, Terra, serves up dishes that celebrate local ingredients, and you can even join in on art classes or guided hikes to discover the landscape. For travelers on a budget, look out for deals during the off-season, typically in the cooler months when rates drop.

Bishop's Lodge, Auberge Resorts Collection, located at 1297 Bishop's Lodge Rd, is another stunning property offering a blend of history and modern luxury. This lodge has been recently renovated, keeping its historical charm while offering the comforts of contemporary living. Just a 15-minute drive from the city center, the lodge feels like a peaceful retreat, surrounded by nature. Guests can explore hiking trails, horseback riding, and even visit the art gallery. To get here, you simply take I-25 and exit onto Bishop's Lodge Road. For a more affordable stay, consider booking a package that includes meals and activities, as these often offer better value.

La Posada de Santa Fe, located at 330 E Palace Ave, is another excellent choice. This elegant hotel feels like a sanctuary right in the heart of the city. Known for its art collection and lush gardens, it offers a unique blend of luxury and artistic ambiance. You can easily walk from here to Santa Fe Plaza, where you can explore galleries, museums, and shops. For those on a budget, check for specials and packages, as they often offer discounted rates during the shoulder seasons. The hotel's restaurant, The Patio Restaurant, is a great place to unwind with some delicious Southwestern cuisine after a day of exploring.

If boutique hotels are more your style, there are several hidden gems that will make your stay in Santa Fe feel intimate and special. The Inn of the Five Graces, located at 150 E De Vargas St, is an upscale boutique hotel that offers luxurious rooms with a mix of Southwestern and Eastern influences. Its location, just a short walk from the Plaza, means you can easily explore the historic district. The attention to detail in the rooms, including fireplaces and unique handcrafted furnishings, makes this place truly memorable. While it's a pricier option, you can sometimes find deals in the off-season, so keep an eye on the website for promotions.

Rosewood Inn of the Anasazi, at 113 Washington Ave, offers a beautiful blend of modern luxury with a deep respect for Native American heritage. This boutique hotel, a short stroll from the Plaza, is known for its incredible service and refined atmosphere. The hotel's on-site restaurant is one of the best in the city, offering sophisticated dishes with a Southwestern twist. To get there, simply head towards the historic Plaza area. If you're looking for an affordable option, consider booking during the off-peak months of spring or fall, as the rates can be more affordable.

El Rey Court, located at 1862 Cerrillos Rd, is a charming and slightly more budget-friendly option compared to the others. This vintage motor lodge, which has been lovingly restored, gives you a taste of old Santa Fe with modern amenities. It's a little further out from the city center, but it's still close enough to downtown for easy access. The rooms have a retro feel, with a laid-back, desert-inspired design. There's also a lovely courtyard with a pool where you can relax after a day of sightseeing. For travelers looking to save, El Rey Court offers some of the best rates in Santa Fe without compromising on character or comfort.

Santa Fe has a way of offering both luxury and comfort, no matter your budget. For those splurging on a stay at a resort, these properties offer incredible experiences, from stunning views to top-notch service and unforgettable activities. But if you're traveling on a budget, there are still plenty of opportunities to experience the charm of Santa Fe, especially if you plan ahead and look for deals in the off-season. Keep in mind that booking directly with the hotels often results in the best rates and most personalized service. Enjoy your stay in this captivating city, where each place you stay only adds to the magic of your experience.

Charming Bed and Breakfasts

Santa Fe's bed and breakfasts offer a cozy, intimate way to experience the city's charm. These spots are perfect for travelers who want a more personal, homey touch to their stay. Whether you're visiting for a romantic getaway, a family trip, or just a solo retreat, these bed and breakfasts provide comfort, warmth, and a genuine connection to the culture of Santa Fe.

El Farolito Bed & Breakfast Inn, located at 514 Galisteo St, is a delightful and intimate place to stay. It's just a short walk from the downtown area, so you're close to all the major attractions, galleries, and restaurants. The inn is set in a beautifully restored adobe building, with cozy rooms that feature traditional Santa Fe-style décor. Guests are treated to a delicious breakfast each morning, with a mix of freshly baked pastries, fruits, and hot dishes to start your day right. To get there, simply head south on Galisteo Street from the Santa Fe Plaza. The owners make you feel like part of the family, and their attention to detail really stands out. If you're on a budget, look for deals during off-peak seasons or check for any special offers, as this place provides great value for the comfort and location.

Casa Culinaria - The Gourmet Inn, located at 913 Kearney Ave, is another charming bed and breakfast that stands out for its culinary offerings. This place is perfect for food lovers, as the owner and chef prepares gourmet breakfasts using fresh, local ingredients. Situated just a few minutes from the Plaza, it's a great base for exploring Santa Fe's rich food scene and cultural sites. You can walk to nearby museums or take a short drive to the beautiful Santa Fe National Forest for a day of hiking. The inn's rooms are comfortable and thoughtfully decorated with a mix of rustic and contemporary elements. To get there, take a left on Kearney Avenue from the Plaza and follow the winding streets. For budget-conscious travelers, Casa Culinaria is a fantastic choice, especially if you're looking for value combined with a memorable, delicious experience each morning.

The Inn on the Alameda, located at 303 E Alameda St, offers a perfect blend of comfort and location. This bed and breakfast is set just a few steps from the Santa Fe River and a short walk from the heart of downtown, making it an ideal spot to explore the city on foot. The rooms are spacious and elegantly designed, with many offering views of the river or the surrounding landscape. Guests can relax in the inn's tranquil courtyard or enjoy a relaxing dip in the outdoor hot tub. Breakfast is served daily, with a focus on locally sourced ingredients. To get here, take a left off of the Santa Fe Plaza onto Alameda Street and continue east. The Inn on the Alameda is perfect for those who want to be close to the action but still enjoy a peaceful and quiet retreat. For budget travelers, the inn often offers discounted rates for extended stays or off-season bookings, so it's worth checking for deals.

Inn of the Turquoise Bear, located at 342 East Buena Vista St, offers an old-world charm and a unique historic touch. This inn is set in a historic adobe house that once belonged to a famous Santa Fe artist. With a cozy, inviting atmosphere, the rooms at the Turquoise Bear are individually decorated, featuring southwestern décor and beautiful antique furniture. The inn offers a delicious breakfast spread each morning and even provides guests with a wine-and-cheese hour in the evening. It's only a 10-minute walk to the Plaza, so you can easily explore the city's main attractions. To reach the inn, head east on Buena Vista Street, which is just a short distance from the main square. If you're looking for a charming, affordable place with a rich history, this is a great option. The Turquoise Bear often offers specials, especially for longer stays or during the off-peak seasons, making it an excellent choice for those traveling on a budget.

Four Kachinas Inn, located at 510 W San Francisco St, is a small, family-run bed and breakfast known for its warm hospitality and intimate setting. Situated just a few blocks from the Santa Fe Plaza, this inn provides easy access to all the attractions, yet it still offers a peaceful and quiet atmosphere. The rooms are cozy and decorated with traditional New Mexican touches, and the breakfasts are homemade and feature locally sourced ingredients. To get there, walk west from the Plaza down San Francisco Street. Four Kachinas Inn is great for travelers who want to be close to the center of it all but prefer a quieter, more relaxed place to return to after a day of exploring. It's also a wonderful option for budget travelers, as they often have special deals and offer competitive rates for the level of service and comfort they provide.

Santa Fe's bed and breakfasts offer a variety of experiences, from gourmet breakfasts to cozy atmospheres, all set in charming locations that let you enjoy the best of the city. Whether you're seeking a culinary adventure, a quiet retreat, or a place full of history, these bed and breakfasts offer something for everyone. They also provide great value, especially if you book in advance or during the off-season. These intimate stays provide a more personal experience, allowing you to connect with the heart of Santa Fe while also enjoying comfort and warmth.

Budget-Friendly Accommodations

Santa Fe offers plenty of affordable accommodation options for travelers looking to explore the city without breaking the bank. From budget motels to cozy hostels, these places allow you to enjoy Santa Fe's rich culture, history, and natural beauty while keeping costs low.

Motel 6 Santa Fe, NM - Downtown, located at 3310 Cerrillos Rd, is a straightforward and affordable option. It's a short drive to downtown Santa Fe, where you can easily access the Plaza and many of the city's renowned art galleries and restaurants. The motel itself offers simple, clean rooms with the usual amenities such as free Wi-Fi, free coffee, and a TV. It's a no-frills spot, but if you're just looking for a place to rest after a day of sightseeing, it does the job perfectly. To get there, simply head south on Cerrillos Road, and you'll find the motel on your right. If you're on a tight budget, Motel 6 provides great value, especially if you're staying for a night or two. For a budget traveler, this is an excellent base for exploring Santa Fe, offering good proximity to the main attractions without the high price tag.

Econo Lodge Inn & Suites, located at 3752 Cerrillos Rd, is another affordable option that offers a bit more in terms of amenities. With a free breakfast, an outdoor pool, and comfortable rooms, the Econo Lodge provides a great balance between comfort and cost. It's also just a short drive to downtown Santa Fe, so you can quickly reach the city center to explore local museums, shops, and eateries. Getting there is easy by following Cerrillos Road south from the Plaza. This is a great option for those who want a little more comfort than a basic motel, while still sticking to a budget. Travelers on a budget will appreciate the free breakfast and access to the outdoor pool during warmer months, which adds value to your stay.

Coyote South Santa Fe, located at 4301 Cerrillos Rd, offers simple accommodations with southwestern flair. This budget-friendly inn is situated a little farther from the Plaza but still easily accessible by car. It's a peaceful spot with spacious rooms that feature unique décor, creating a cozy atmosphere for guests. The hotel offers essential amenities such as free Wi-Fi and free parking. To get there, head south on Cerrillos Road from the city center. While the location may not be as central as other options, the quiet environment and affordable rates make Coyote South a great choice for budget-conscious travelers. If you're traveling on a tight budget, you can enjoy a peaceful stay without sacrificing comfort, with easy access to nearby shopping and dining.

The Santa Fe Hostel, located at 1424 Cerrillos Rd, is perfect for those looking to meet fellow travelers and experience a more social, communal type of accommodation. The hostel offers both dormitory-style rooms and private rooms at very reasonable rates. It's located just a short drive from the downtown area, and with a bus stop nearby, you can easily get to the Plaza and other attractions. Guests can use the shared kitchen to save on meals, and there's a cozy common area to hang out and relax. Getting to the Santa Fe Hostel is easy by heading south on Cerrillos Road. If you're traveling solo or just want to keep costs low, the hostel offers a fantastic way to meet people and share experiences. Budget travelers will appreciate the affordable rates, shared amenities, and relaxed vibe.

Picacho Peak State Park, located about 20 miles west of Santa Fe at 0 Picacho Peak Rd, offers a great way to experience the outdoors on a budget. The park has a variety of camping options, including tent and RV sites, which provide a more affordable way to stay close to nature. There are beautiful hiking trails and picnic areas, and if you enjoy stargazing, this park is a perfect spot for that too. To get there, simply take I-40 west from Santa Fe, then exit at Picacho Peak Road. For nature lovers or those wanting to get away from the hustle and bustle of the city, Picacho Peak State Park offers a peaceful and budget-friendly option. Camping is an excellent way to experience Santa Fe's natural beauty while keeping expenses low, and the park is perfect for outdoor activities like hiking, bird watching, and stargazing.

Hyde Memorial State Park, located at 740 Hyde Park Rd, is another fantastic spot for budget-conscious travelers who want to connect with nature. Situated in the Santa Fe National Forest, the park offers campsites that are both affordable and scenic. There are hiking trails that wind through the forest, offering views of the surrounding mountains, and during winter, the area is popular for cross-country skiing. To get to Hyde Memorial State Park, drive north on Hyde Park Road, which is a scenic route that leads up to the park. Whether you're camping or just spending the day hiking, the park offers a serene escape at a fraction of the cost of other accommodations in Santa Fe. If you're looking to immerse yourself in nature without spending too much, this is the perfect place to stay.

Santa Fe offers a wide range of budget-friendly accommodations, from motels to hostels and campgrounds, giving travelers the opportunity to experience the city and its surroundings without breaking the bank. Whether you prefer a simple motel room, a social hostel, or a peaceful stay in the great outdoors, there's something for every budget. Keep an eye out for seasonal deals, book in advance when possible, and look for places that offer additional amenities like free parking or breakfast to get the best value for your money. These budget-friendly options are perfect for travelers who want to enjoy all that Santa Fe has to offer without the high cost.

Unique Stays: Adobe Homes and Historic Inns

Santa Fe is a city rich in history and culture, and its adobe homes and historic inns provide an immersive way to experience its charm. Staying in these unique accommodations offers more than a comfortable bed—it's a chance to live the city's heritage, surrounded by traditional architecture, handcrafted furnishings, and a warm Southwestern atmosphere.

La Fonda on the Plaza, located at 100 E San Francisco St, sits at the very heart of Santa Fe's historic downtown. This landmark hotel has stood at the end of the Santa Fe Trail for centuries, making it an iconic destination for travelers. Its adobe-style design, colorful tiles, and Native American artwork create a captivating ambiance. To get there, drive to the Santa Fe Plaza and follow signs for the hotel. Guests can enjoy its luxurious rooms and dine at La Plazuela, the hotel's restaurant, which serves flavorful New Mexican cuisine. Don't miss the rooftop Bell Tower Bar for breathtaking sunset views. La Fonda is perfect for exploring the Plaza's attractions, from boutique shopping to museums. While it's on the higher end of the price spectrum, visiting during the off-season or booking early can sometimes yield discounted rates. Even budget travelers can enjoy the ambiance by stopping in for a meal or drink.

The Inn of the Five Graces, located at 150 E De Vargas St, is a luxurious retreat blending Santa Fe's adobe charm with a global touch. Each room is a masterpiece, adorned with richly woven textiles, hand-carved furniture, and intricate tilework inspired by Central Asian artistry. This inn is just a short walk from the historic Plaza, and its secluded location makes it feel like a peaceful oasis. To get there, head south from the Plaza along De Vargas Street. The inn offers complimentary breakfast and evening turndown service, making it a perfect choice for a romantic or tranquil getaway. Although staying here is a splurge, its exceptional service and one-of-a-kind decor make it unforgettable. If you're on a tighter budget, consider visiting the nearby San Miguel Chapel or taking a stroll through the charming neighborhood to soak in the historic atmosphere.

El Rey Court, located at 1862 Cerrillos Rd, offers a delightful mix of vintage charm and modern comforts. Originally built as a motor court in the 1930s, El Rey has been beautifully restored while maintaining its adobe-style roots. This boutique inn features quirky, eclectic decor and cozy rooms, each with its unique flair. The on-site restaurant and bar, La Reina, is a lively spot to enjoy local craft drinks and live music. To reach El Rey Court, head south on Cerrillos Road from downtown Santa Fe. Its location makes it easy to explore both the city and surrounding attractions, including Meow Wolf's immersive art experience nearby. With reasonable rates compared to high-end inns, El Rey is a fantastic choice for travelers seeking a stylish yet budget-friendly stay. Those on a tighter budget can opt for a standard room and make use of the free parking and on-site amenities.

Each of these unique stays offers an authentic Santa Fe experience, letting you connect with the city's rich heritage and artistic spirit. Whether you're drawn to the luxury and history of La Fonda, the global elegance of the Inn of the Five Graces, or the retro-chic vibe of El Rey Court, you'll find a memorable escape. Travelers on a budget can still enjoy the essence of these places by timing their visits strategically, exploring nearby landmarks, or simply soaking in the vibrant atmosphere of Santa Fe's adobe architecture. These accommodations aren't just places to sleep—they're windows into the soul of Santa Fe.

CHAPTER 4.
SANTA FE'S VIBRANT NEIGHBORHOODS

Historic Downtown and the Plaza

Historic Downtown Santa Fe and the Plaza is the heart of the city's charm and culture. This area offers an enchanting blend of history, art, and local life that makes it a must-visit destination for anyone traveling to the region. Walking through the narrow streets lined with adobe buildings and shaded by cottonwood trees feels like stepping back in time, yet the vibrant energy of shops, galleries, and eateries keeps it alive and modern.

The Plaza itself is a central square surrounded by historic landmarks, boutique stores, and art galleries. It has been the gathering place of Santa Fe for over 400 years, making it one of the oldest public spaces in the United States. The Palace of the Governors, located along one side, is a National Historic Landmark and an incredible spot to explore. Its shaded portal hosts Native American artisans who sell handmade jewelry, pottery, and other crafts, providing an authentic way to bring home a piece of the region's artistry.

You'll also find the Cathedral Basilica of St. Francis of Assisi just a short walk from the Plaza. Its impressive Romanesque Revival architecture is a striking contrast to the adobe surroundings, and stepping inside reveals serene beauty with colorful stained glass windows and intricate details. Nearby, the Loretto Chapel is home to the famous "Miraculous Staircase," a spiraling wooden staircase that attracts visitors and admirers of its mysterious construction.

Art lovers will feel right at home in the area. The Georgia O'Keeffe Museum, located a few blocks from the Plaza, celebrates the work of this iconic artist whose paintings capture the essence of New Mexico's landscapes. For a more immersive experience, wander through the many art galleries that dot the streets, each offering unique pieces from local and international artists.

Shopping around the Plaza is a joy, whether you're looking for high-quality jewelry, Southwestern-style clothing, or handmade crafts. Stores like Shiprock Santa Fe and the Spanish Market provide opportunities to discover authentic and creative pieces. Don't forget to explore the Santa Fe Farmers Market if you're in town on a Saturday—it's a colorful, bustling spot filled with local produce, baked goods, and artisan products.

Dining in the Plaza area is equally memorable. You'll find a mix of fine dining and casual eateries that serve delicious New Mexican cuisine, blending Pueblo and Spanish influences. The red and green chile, staples of local cooking, are not to be missed. Restaurants like The Shed and La Plazuela offer traditional dishes in warm, welcoming settings, while casual spots such as Tia Sophia's are perfect for a hearty breakfast burrito.

The best way to enjoy the Plaza and downtown is on foot. Park your car or arrive via a local bus and take your time exploring. The area is compact, and strolling its streets reveals hidden courtyards, fountains, and gardens. Evenings are particularly magical, as the setting sun bathes the adobe buildings in a warm glow, and musicians or performers often entertain visitors in the Plaza.

For travelers on a budget, there are plenty of ways to enjoy the area without overspending. Many of the landmarks, like the Cathedral Basilica and the Palace of the Governors' portal, are free to visit. Browsing the galleries and Native American crafts doesn't cost a thing unless you're tempted to take something home. The Plaza also has benches and grassy areas that are perfect for a picnic lunch or simply relaxing while soaking up the lively atmosphere.

Historic Downtown Santa Fe and the Plaza are where the city's past and present come together. Every corner tells a story, from the centuries-old adobe walls to the vibrant displays of modern art and culture. It's a place to wander, discover, and feel the soul of Santa Fe, creating memories that will stay with you long after you leave.

Canyon Road: The Art District

Canyon Road in Santa Fe is a world-renowned art district that feels like an open-air gallery brimming with creativity, history, and culture. Just a short distance from the historic downtown, this charming road stretches for about a mile and is home to over a hundred art galleries, studios, boutiques, and cafes. Walking along Canyon Road is an experience that immerses you in the vibrant art scene of Santa Fe, blending traditional Southwestern styles with contemporary works from local and international artists.

The moment you step onto Canyon Road, you're greeted by its unique atmosphere. Adobe buildings, many of them historic, are nestled among colorful gardens and shaded by trees, creating a setting that's as artistic as the works displayed inside. The galleries here showcase an incredible range of art forms, from classic paintings and Native American pottery to modern sculptures and avant-garde installations. You'll find something to captivate every artistic taste, whether you're a serious collector or simply exploring out of curiosity.

One of the joys of visiting Canyon Road is the opportunity to meet the artists. Many galleries are owner-operated or host artists in residence, giving you a chance to hear the stories behind the creations. Engaging in conversation with them adds a personal connection to the pieces you admire, making the visit all the more enriching. Some galleries even offer live demonstrations, allowing you to see the creative process in action.

Beyond the galleries, Canyon Road is also a feast for the senses with its mix of boutiques and specialty shops. From handmade jewelry and textiles to unique home decor and antiques, the shops here offer treasures you won't find anywhere else. If you're looking for a special souvenir or gift, this is the perfect place to explore.

As you wander, take time to enjoy the peaceful ambiance of the area. Many galleries have courtyards or outdoor displays where you can pause and take in the surroundings. The slow pace of Canyon Road encourages you to linger and truly soak up its charm. Even if you're not planning to buy, the sheer variety and quality of the art on display make it a worthwhile visit.

Food and drink are also an essential part of the Canyon Road experience. Small cafes and restaurants dot the road, offering everything from gourmet meals to quick snacks. Many of them have outdoor seating, where you can relax with a cup of coffee or a glass of wine while enjoying the artistic vibe. Places like The Compound and El Farol are favorites among visitors for their delicious cuisine and inviting atmosphere.

The best way to explore Canyon Road is on foot. Parking can be limited, especially during peak times, so consider leaving your car downtown and walking or taking a short ride-share or local shuttle. Comfortable shoes are a must, as you'll want to spend hours meandering through the galleries and shops.

If you're visiting on a Friday evening, you might catch an art walk or special event. These gatherings bring the community together and often include live music, refreshments, and extended gallery hours. It's a festive way to experience the road and connect with other art enthusiasts.

For travelers on a budget, Canyon Road still offers plenty to enjoy. Browsing the galleries and outdoor installations is completely free, and many galleries are happy to share their stories even if you're not purchasing. You can pack a picnic or grab a reasonably priced snack from one of the cafes to keep costs down while still soaking in the unique atmosphere.

Canyon Road is more than just a destination; it's an experience that captures the creative spirit of Santa Fe. Whether you're admiring the art, meeting the artists, shopping for a one-of-a-kind piece, or simply enjoying the beauty of the adobe-lined street, it's a place that invites you to slow down and appreciate the artistry in every detail.

Railyard and Guadalupe Districts

The Railyard and Guadalupe Districts in Santa Fe are two lively and dynamic areas that showcase the city's contemporary side while staying true to its rich cultural heritage. Located just a short walk or drive from the historic downtown, these neighborhoods offer a mix of art, shopping, dining, and entertainment that makes them perfect for a day of exploration.

The Railyard District gets its name from its historical roots as a hub for train travel. Today, it has been transformed into a vibrant gathering place while still retaining its industrial charm. At the heart of the district is the Santa Fe Farmers' Market, a must-visit for anyone who loves fresh, locally sourced food. On market days, you'll find colorful stalls overflowing with fruits, vegetables, baked goods, and handmade products. The lively atmosphere is made even better by live music and the friendly chatter of locals and visitors.

Art lovers will feel right at home in the Railyard District. This area is home to several contemporary galleries, including SITE Santa Fe, an internationally recognized venue for modern art exhibitions. The blend of cutting-edge works and innovative installations makes it a fascinating stop. You can also find pop-up galleries and open studios, giving you a glimpse into Santa Fe's thriving creative community.

The Railyard Park is a welcoming green space where you can relax and enjoy the outdoors. With its walking trails, playgrounds, and art installations, it's an excellent spot to unwind. During the warmer months, the park hosts events like concerts, outdoor movies, and festivals, adding to the lively energy of the district.

Not far from the Railyard, the Guadalupe District offers a charming mix of old and new. This neighborhood is named after the historic Santuario de Guadalupe, a beautiful adobe church adorned with stunning religious artwork. It's worth stopping by to admire the serene atmosphere and intricate details of this iconic landmark.

The Guadalupe District is also known for its unique shops and boutiques. Strolling along the tree-lined streets, you'll discover stores selling everything from handcrafted jewelry and Southwestern home decor to clothing and vintage finds. It's a treasure hunt for those looking to take home something special.

When it's time to eat, both districts have an abundance of options. The Railyard is dotted with trendy cafes and eateries serving everything from farm-to-table meals to international cuisine. The Guadalupe District offers a mix of family-owned restaurants and hip dining spots where you can sample local flavors, including New Mexican staples like green chile enchiladas and tamales. Whether you're in the mood for a quick coffee or a leisurely dinner, you'll find plenty to satisfy your cravings.

Getting to these districts is easy. The Railyard District is accessible by car, with ample parking available, or by taking the Rail Runner Express train, which stops right in the heart of the area. The Guadalupe District is close enough to downtown Santa Fe that you can walk or take a short ride-share trip. Both areas are pedestrian-friendly, making it easy to explore at your own pace.

For travelers on a budget, these districts offer many affordable and free activities. Browsing the farmers' market or galleries costs nothing unless you choose to buy, and the parks provide a peaceful setting for a picnic or a leisurely stroll. Many restaurants offer reasonably priced menus, so you can enjoy a delicious meal without overspending.

The Railyard and Guadalupe Districts provide a wonderful contrast to the historic charm of downtown Santa Fe. With their contemporary vibe, diverse attractions, and welcoming atmosphere, they offer a fresh perspective on the city while staying connected to its roots. Whether you're shopping for unique items, savoring local cuisine, or simply soaking in the vibrant energy, these neighborhoods promise a memorable experience.

Tesuque Village and Surrounding Areas

Tesuque Village, a picturesque hamlet just a short drive north of Santa Fe, is a peaceful escape that captures the charm of Northern New Mexico. Surrounded by rolling hills, lush cottonwoods, and the majestic Sangre de Cristo Mountains, this small community feels like stepping into a tranquil oasis. Its quiet atmosphere, artistic heritage, and natural beauty make it a wonderful destination for a day trip or a serene getaway.

The heart of Tesuque is its small yet inviting village center. As you wander through, you'll notice a mix of historic adobe homes and modern architectural touches, all blending seamlessly with the landscape. One of the must-visit spots here is the Tesuque Village Market, a beloved local gathering place that doubles as a casual eatery and general store.

Whether you're stopping in for a freshly baked pastry, a flavorful wood-fired pizza, or a cup of strong coffee, the warm and friendly atmosphere makes it feel like a home away from home.

Art is a significant part of life in Tesuque. The village and its surrounding areas are dotted with artist studios and galleries where you can discover unique works inspired by the region's culture and scenery. The Shidoni Foundry and Galleries, just outside the village, is particularly noteworthy. This sprawling outdoor sculpture garden features stunning bronze pieces set against the dramatic backdrop of the mountains. Watching artisans work in the foundry is a fascinating experience, offering insight into the intricate process of metal casting.

Nature enthusiasts will find plenty to love in and around Tesuque. The Tesuque Pueblo, located nearby, is a place of cultural significance and natural beauty. Although access may be limited for visitors, the area's scenic surroundings and the chance to learn about the Pueblo's traditions are deeply enriching. For a more immersive outdoor experience, the trails around Tesuque Creek provide a refreshing retreat. These paths wind through shaded forests and open meadows, perfect for hiking, picnicking, or simply soaking in the serenity.

Not far from the village, you'll find the Santa Fe Opera, a world-renowned venue that blends high culture with breathtaking views. During the summer season, you can catch performances that range from classic operas to contemporary works, all staged in the open-air amphitheater. Arriving early for a tailgate picnic in the parking lot—a cherished local tradition—adds to the magic of an evening at the opera.

Reaching Tesuque is easy. From downtown Santa Fe, it's a scenic ten-minute drive along Bishop's Lodge Road or Highway 285. If you're without a car, rideshares and local taxi services are convenient options. The short journey feels like a step back in time, as the road winds through landscapes that evoke the region's timeless allure.

For travelers on a budget, Tesuque offers many simple pleasures that don't require spending much. Exploring the trails, browsing the art at Shidoni, or relaxing at the village market are all enjoyable ways to experience the area. Packing a picnic to enjoy by Tesuque Creek is another delightful and cost-effective option.

Tesuque and its surrounding areas offer a harmonious blend of quiet beauty, artistic inspiration, and cultural depth. Whether you're seeking a day of relaxation, a touch of creativity, or an escape into nature, this charming village delivers a peaceful experience just minutes from the bustling streets of Santa Fe.

CHAPTER 5.
CULTURAL EXPERIENCES
Art Galleries and Studios

Santa Fe is a haven for art lovers, and its art galleries and studios are at the heart of this vibrant creative scene. With its rich cultural heritage and breathtaking landscapes, the city has inspired artists for generations, and visitors are spoiled for choice when it comes to exploring unique and extraordinary works of art.

One of the most iconic places to begin is Canyon Road, where art seems to spill out of every doorway and into the street. This historic lane is home to more than 100 galleries, featuring everything from traditional Native American pottery and textiles to contemporary sculptures and vibrant abstract paintings. Walking along Canyon Road feels like stepping into an open-air museum, with the charming adobe buildings adding to the atmosphere. Many of the galleries, like the Blue Rain Gallery and Nedra Matteucci Galleries, are welcoming and encourage visitors to take their time exploring.

For a more modern experience, the Railyard Arts District is a must-visit. This trendy area showcases contemporary and experimental works in spaces like SITE Santa Fe, an internationally renowned contemporary art space that often hosts cutting-edge exhibitions and thought-provoking installations. The Railyard is also home to smaller studios where you can meet artists at work and learn about their creative processes. The vibe here is youthful and dynamic, offering a fresh perspective on Santa Fe's art scene.

If you're looking for a more intimate and personalized art experience, visit the numerous independent studios scattered across the city. Many local artists open their doors to visitors, offering a behind-the-scenes look at their work. It's an incredible opportunity to see creativity in action, whether it's a painter perfecting their latest piece or a jeweler crafting intricate designs. A visit to the studios in Tesuque, just outside Santa Fe, combines this artistic experience with a peaceful rural setting.

The Lensic Performing Arts Center often features exhibitions alongside its live performances, offering a blend of visual and performing arts. For those interested in Native American art, the Wheelwright Museum of the American Indian and the Museum of Indian Arts & Culture provide insight into the traditions and evolution of indigenous art forms. These museums often collaborate with local galleries, creating a well-rounded art journey across the city.

Art in Santa Fe isn't confined to galleries and studios. Public art installations and murals can be found in many neighborhoods, reflecting the city's rich cultural tapestry. The Santa Fe Plaza and the surrounding streets are excellent spots for discovering sculptures and outdoor exhibits, often with historical significance.

Reaching these galleries and studios is straightforward. Canyon Road is a short walk or drive from downtown Santa

Fe, while the Railyard Arts District is easily accessible by car or public transport. Many studios and galleries offer free admission, making it a budget-friendly activity. Some even host special events, like gallery openings or artist talks, where you can mingle with the creative community.

When planning your visit, allow plenty of time to explore at your own pace. Art in Santa Fe is deeply personal and diverse, and every piece tells a story. Taking the time to connect with these works—whether through a guided tour, a conversation with an artist, or simply wandering through the galleries—makes the experience truly memorable.

Santa Fe's art scene is a vibrant reflection of its unique identity, blending history, innovation, and boundless creativity. Whether you're a seasoned collector or just curious about art, the galleries and studios here offer something special for everyone.

Museums to Explore

Santa Fe's museums are a treasure trove of culture and history, offering a window into the rich artistic and cultural heritage of the Southwest. Two standouts in the city are the Georgia O'Keeffe Museum and the Museum of Indian Arts and Culture, each providing a unique and immersive experience.

The Georgia O'Keeffe Museum is located at 217 Johnson Street, right in the heart of downtown Santa Fe. It's easily accessible by foot if you're staying nearby, or a short drive with convenient parking available in the area. Dedicated to the life and work of one of America's most celebrated artists, this museum is a must-see for anyone drawn to the vibrant landscapes and delicate flowers of the Southwest. Stepping inside, you're greeted by a serene atmosphere, where O'Keeffe's iconic paintings take center stage. Her works are displayed thoughtfully, allowing you to see how her art evolved over the years.

As you wander through the galleries, the museum offers insight into O'Keeffe's life, with personal items, sketches, and photographs providing context for her artistic journey. One highlight is her depiction of the New Mexico landscape, which captures the region's stark beauty in a way that feels both timeless and deeply personal. Be sure to check out any temporary exhibitions, as the museum frequently hosts rotating collections that complement O'Keeffe's work. To make the most of your visit, consider joining a guided tour or downloading the museum's app for additional context and stories about the pieces on display.

Not far from the Georgia O'Keeffe Museum is the Museum of Indian Arts and Culture, located at 710 Camino Lejo on Museum Hill. It's about a 10-minute drive from downtown Santa Fe, and you can reach it by car or the city's shuttle service, which is a budget-friendly option. The museum sits in a tranquil setting, with sweeping views of the surrounding landscape that set the stage for the journey you're about to take into Native American history and art.

Inside, the museum showcases an extensive collection of artifacts, from intricate beadwork and pottery to ceremonial garments and tools. Each piece tells a story of the diverse Native American tribes that have called the region home for centuries. The permanent exhibition, "Here, Now and Always," is a highlight, weaving together personal narratives, historical accounts, and artistic expressions to create a deeply moving experience. Interactive displays make the museum engaging for all ages, and you'll leave with a newfound appreciation for the resilience and creativity of these cultures.

To enhance your visit, plan to participate in one of the museum's workshops or lectures, which delve deeper into specific aspects of Native American traditions. The outdoor sculpture garden is another gem, perfect for a peaceful stroll as you reflect on what you've seen inside. The museum's shop is an excellent place to find unique gifts, with handcrafted jewelry, pottery, and books that support local artists and artisans.

Both museums offer more than just art and history—they provide a sense of connection to the spirit of Santa Fe. They're places to pause and absorb the beauty and complexity of the world around you. For travelers on a budget, keep an eye out for discounted admission days or free entry times, often available to New Mexico residents or through special promotions. Packing a light snack and water can help you enjoy Museum Hill's peaceful surroundings without needing to leave the area for a meal.

Santa Fe's museums aren't just places to visit; they're experiences to savor. They allow you to step into the stories, landscapes, and traditions that make this city so unique, offering something for the curious and creative alike. With a little planning, they'll leave you inspired and ready to explore more of what Santa Fe has to offer.

The Santa Fe Opera: A Summer Spectacle

The Santa Fe Opera is a dazzling summer experience that captures the imagination of everyone who visits. Perched on a hilltop just a short drive north of Santa Fe, it offers not only world-class performances but also stunning views of the surrounding desert and mountains. Located at 301 Opera Drive, the venue is about 10 miles from downtown Santa Fe, and it's easy to get there by car. If you don't have a vehicle, local taxi services or ride-sharing apps are convenient options.

As you approach the open-air theater, the design of the building immediately impresses. Its architecture blends seamlessly with the natural landscape, and the setting sun often provides a dramatic backdrop before the show begins. Arriving early is highly recommended, not only to soak in the views but also to enjoy one of the opera's beloved traditions:

tailgating. Here, you'll find opera-goers setting up elaborate picnics with gourmet spreads and wine, making the pre-show atmosphere lively and unique. Even if you don't participate, it's worth walking through the parking lot to take in the festive scene.

The performances themselves are nothing short of spectacular. The Santa Fe Opera is known for its diverse repertoire, which includes classic operas by composers like Mozart and Verdi, as well as modern and rarely performed works. The acoustics of the theater are impeccable, and the open-air design allows the evening breeze to mingle with the music, creating a magical experience. English subtitles are provided, ensuring that even newcomers to opera can follow the storylines and enjoy the performances.

If you're visiting for the first time, consider attending one of the pre-performance talks, which provide an engaging introduction to the opera you're about to see. These sessions are held on-site and are free with your ticket. They're especially helpful if you're unfamiliar with opera, as they highlight key themes, characters, and moments to watch for.

The opera's location also lends itself to memorable evenings under the stars. The roof of the theater is open at the sides, offering views of the expansive night sky. As the performances unfold, you'll often catch glimpses of constellations or even the occasional shooting star, adding another layer of enchantment to the experience.

Tickets range in price, and there are options to suit various budgets. For travelers looking to save, the less expensive seats still offer excellent views and allow you to fully enjoy the acoustics. Booking well in advance is advisable, as performances often sell out quickly, especially for popular productions. Discounts for students and young adults are sometimes available, so be sure to check the opera's website or inquire at the box office.

Dress code at the Santa Fe Opera is another aspect that adds to its charm. While some patrons embrace the opportunity to dress elegantly, others opt for more casual attire, reflecting the laid-back yet sophisticated vibe of the event. Comfortable shoes are a good idea, as there's some walking involved from the parking area to the theater.

Attending the Santa Fe Opera is more than just a night out—it's an unforgettable experience that combines the best of music, culture, and nature. Whether you're a seasoned opera lover or a curious first-timer, the combination of world-class performances and breathtaking scenery is sure to leave a lasting impression. It's one of those rare events where you feel both transported by the art on stage and deeply connected to the beauty of Santa Fe.

Traditional Native American Markets

Exploring the traditional Native American markets in Santa Fe is like stepping into a vibrant tapestry of culture, history, and artistry. These markets are a cornerstone of the city's identity, offering visitors the chance to connect with Indigenous traditions through handmade crafts, jewelry, and art. They are not just places to shop but immersive experiences where stories, skills, and heritage come to life.

The most iconic of these markets is the Native American Vendors Program at the Palace of the Governors, located right in the heart of Santa Fe Plaza. Here, under the shaded portal of this historic building, you'll find rows of artisans displaying their work on colorful blankets. The atmosphere is warm and inviting, with artists eager to share the inspiration and techniques behind their creations. From intricate silver and turquoise jewelry to beautifully crafted pottery and woven textiles, every piece tells a story. Because each artisan must meet strict standards to sell here, you can be assured of the authenticity and quality of what you're buying.

The best way to enjoy this market is to arrive early in the day when the selection is freshest and the atmosphere still has a calm, morning energy. Take your time to browse, ask questions, and learn about the cultural significance of the items. Many of the artisans are happy to explain how their work is tied to their heritage, making your purchases not just souvenirs but meaningful keepsakes.

Santa Fe also hosts larger events celebrating Native American art, such as the Santa Fe Indian Market, held annually in

August. This massive gathering transforms the downtown area into a bustling hub of creativity, with hundreds of artists from across the country showcasing their work. The market is not only about buying art; it's an experience filled with music, dance, and food that immerses you in Native culture. Be sure to explore the variety of booths and attend demonstrations to see traditional techniques in action, like beadwork, pottery-making, and weaving.

Another gem to explore is the Tesuque Pueblo Flea Market, located just a short drive north of Santa Fe. While smaller and less formal than the Plaza market, it offers an eclectic mix of Native American crafts, vintage finds, and unique treasures from various cultures. The setting itself is charming, with a relaxed vibe that encourages browsing at your own pace. Here, you can find one-of-a-kind items at reasonable prices, making it an excellent choice for travelers on a budget.

For those interested in deeper cultural connections, the Indian Arts Research Center at the School for Advanced Research often collaborates with local Native artisans to host special exhibitions and sales. These events are a wonderful opportunity to view and purchase museum-quality pieces while supporting Indigenous artists directly.

To make the most of your visit to these markets, it's important to come with an open mind and a willingness to engage. Bargaining is not customary in many Native markets, as the prices reflect the time, skill, and cultural value invested in the work. Instead, appreciate the artistry and consider the cultural support your purchases provide. If you're on a budget, smaller items like earrings, prints, or mini pottery pieces can still carry the essence of the artist's work and heritage.

Visiting these markets isn't just about shopping; it's about experiencing the rich traditions of the Southwest. Whether you're strolling through the Plaza, exploring the Tesuque Flea Market, or attending a major event like the Indian Market, you'll feel a deep connection to the spirit of Santa Fe. Each visit is a chance to honor the vibrant cultures that have shaped this unique city, and you'll leave with memories and treasures that resonate far beyond your time here.

Santa Fe Events and Festivals

Santa Fe is a city alive with celebrations, from its rich cultural heritage to its vibrant arts scene. Here are some of the most notable festivals and events in Santa Fe, each offering a unique window into the city's traditions, creativity, and spirit.

Santa Fe Indian Market
Held every August, this world-renowned event coincides with the peak of summer when Santa Fe is bathed in warm sunlight and its skies are an uninterrupted canvas of blue. The lively season heightens the festival's energy, with streets filled with art, culture, and a palpable sense of community. The climate is perfect for strolling through outdoor exhibits in the heart of the historic Plaza.

Cultural Significance: The Indian Market celebrates Native American art, showcasing the works of over 1,000 Indigenous artists from across North America. It represents a century-old tradition and is a cornerstone of the Santa Fe cultural calendar. Visitors witness the continuation of ancient artistic practices, from pottery and jewelry-making to painting and textiles, with each piece carrying its own cultural narrative.

Activities and Attractions: Art enthusiasts can browse countless booths featuring exquisite handmade pieces, often with the chance to meet the artists. Live performances include traditional dances, storytelling, and contemporary music. Culinary offerings feature Native-inspired dishes like fry bread and blue corn specialties. The event also includes a juried art competition, fashion shows, and auctions, adding layers of excitement.

Practical Tips: Arrive early to secure parking and avoid the mid-day crowds. Wear comfortable shoes for walking and a wide-brimmed hat for shade. Accommodations in Santa Fe fill up quickly during this time, so book well in advance.

Cost Considerations: Entry is generally free for browsing the market, but prices for art vary widely, from affordable prints to high-value collector's pieces. Budget-conscious visitors can enjoy free performances and smaller, more affordable souvenirs.

Crowd Management: The market is busiest on Saturday mornings, so visiting later in the afternoon or on Sunday can offer a more relaxed experience. The early bird often finds the best art selections, while latecomers enjoy a more serene atmosphere.

Comparative Insights: As the largest Native American art market globally, it surpasses similar events in scale and prestige, offering unparalleled access to master artists and cultural immersion.

Santa Fe Fiesta

The Santa Fe Fiesta takes place each September, celebrating the city's autumn charm. As the temperatures cool and the aspens begin to turn golden, the crisp air lends a festive energy to this centuries-old event.

Cultural Significance: This is the oldest civic celebration in the United States, commemorating the Spanish reconquest of Santa Fe in 1692. It blends Catholic traditions, Indigenous influences, and Spanish heritage, creating a truly unique cultural mosaic. Central to the Fiesta are the rituals of La Entrada de Don Diego de Vargas and the burning of Zozobra, a giant puppet symbolizing gloom.

Activities and Attractions: The Fiesta features parades, musical performances, and traditional dances, often accompanied by delicious food like tamales and biscochitos. The burning of Zozobra is a dramatic spectacle that draws large crowds, symbolizing renewal and letting go of past worries. Other highlights include arts and crafts markets and a carnival atmosphere throughout the Plaza.

Practical Tips: Dress in layers to accommodate cooler evenings and bring a light blanket if attending the Zozobra event. Arrive early for parades and ceremonies to secure good viewing spots.

Cost Considerations: Many events are free, though there are ticket fees for Zozobra and other special activities. Food and vendor prices are generally reasonable, and exploring on a budget is possible by prioritizing free performances and activities.

Crowd Management: Zozobra attracts the largest crowds, so plan to arrive hours early or choose less congested events during the Fiesta. Public transportation or rideshares can help avoid parking hassles.

Comparative Insights: While similar in spirit to other Hispanic heritage festivals, Santa Fe Fiesta's deep historical roots and blend of cultures make it uniquely authentic and emotionally resonant.

Santa Fe International Folk Art Market
Held every July, this event coincides with Santa Fe's summer bloom, when gardens are vibrant and outdoor events thrive. The warm, sunny days create a perfect backdrop for exploring this vibrant global marketplace.

Cultural Significance: This market is a celebration of global cultures, with artists from over 50 countries coming together to share their crafts. It emphasizes sustainable livelihoods and cultural preservation, making it a meaningful experience for both visitors and participants.

Activities and Attractions: The market is filled with colorful booths offering textiles, jewelry, and sculptures, all made by hand. Live music, cultural performances, and storytelling create a lively, immersive atmosphere. Many artists demonstrate their techniques, giving insight into their craftsmanship.

Practical Tips: Wear comfortable clothing and bring a reusable water bottle to stay hydrated. Tickets for early access provide a quieter shopping experience. Bring cash, as not all vendors accept credit cards, and pack light for ease of movement.

Cost Considerations: Entry fees vary, with early-bird tickets offering premium access. While some crafts are high-end, many affordable options allow visitors to take home a piece of global artistry.

Crowd Management: Early hours are less crowded, while afternoons bring a festive bustle. Arriving early ensures you can interact with artists before the crowds gather.

Comparative Insights: Unlike local artisan fairs, this market's international scope sets it apart, offering a rare chance to experience global cultures in one place.

These festivals and events showcase Santa Fe's rich cultural tapestry, each offering its own unique experiences and opportunities to connect with the city's heritage and community. Whether you're an art lover, history buff, or casual traveler, these celebrations provide unforgettable memories and a deeper appreciation of Santa Fe's spirit.

CHAPTER 6.
LANDMARKS AND ATTRACTIONS
The Historic Santa Fe Plaza

The Historic Santa Fe Plaza is the beating heart of the city, an area steeped in history, culture, and vibrant energy. Located at 63 Lincoln Avenue, the Plaza has served as a central gathering spot for over 400 years, and it continues to be a hub for both locals and travelers alike. As soon as you step onto the Plaza, you're instantly transported into a blend of old-world charm and modern-day bustle. Whether you're coming for the art, the food, or simply to soak in the atmosphere, there's something here for everyone.

Getting to the Plaza is easy, and it's right in the center of the city. If you're staying in Santa Fe, you can easily walk there from many hotels or restaurants. If you're coming from farther out, there are plenty of parking options around the Plaza, but be aware that it can get busy, especially during festivals or weekends. Santa Fe's bus system also has stops near the Plaza, making it an accessible destination even if you're not driving.

One of the best parts of visiting the Plaza is that you can enjoy it without paying any entrance fee. The atmosphere alone is worth the visit. You can spend time browsing the historic architecture, from the adobe-style buildings to the iconic St. Francis Cathedral, which stands on the north side of the Plaza. The cathedral is a must-see for anyone interested in history or architecture. Inside, the stained-glass windows and the soft light that filters through give the place a peaceful, reverent feel.

For me, every visit to the Plaza is about the experience of being there, of walking around and feeling connected to Santa Fe's past. One of the things I love most is the vibrant market atmosphere. Local artisans and vendors set up shop in the Plaza selling everything from beautiful Native American jewelry to hand-painted pottery. If you're lucky, you'll catch one of the traditional dance performances or a live music set that fills the air with local sounds, adding a lively backdrop to the scene.

There's also a great deal of history to absorb. Many of the buildings around the Plaza date back to the Spanish colonial era, and a walk through the area feels like stepping into a living museum. If you're interested in learning more about the history, you can visit the New Mexico History Museum located just off the Plaza. It's a great spot to learn about Santa Fe's roots, from its early days as a Native American settlement to its role as a Spanish outpost and beyond. The museum is free to enter on Sundays, and even if you're just walking around, the beautiful courtyards and sculptures are worth a visit.

As for dining, you'll find a variety of options around the Plaza. One of my favorites is the famous Plaza Café, a perfect spot for a hearty breakfast or a relaxed lunch with a view of the square. The food here feels like an extension of Santa Fe itself – rich, flavorful, and infused with local culture. Whether you're in the mood for classic New Mexican dishes like enchiladas and tamales, or you prefer something lighter like fresh salads, you'll find plenty of options.

If you want to make the most of your time in the Plaza, I recommend arriving early in the day before it gets crowded. The mornings are peaceful, and you can take a leisurely stroll around the Plaza before the rush of tourists and locals fills the area. And if you're there on a weekend, don't miss the Santa Fe Farmers Market, which is just a short walk away in the Railyard District. It's a great spot to pick up fresh produce, artisanal goods, and souvenirs.

When it comes to crowd management, the Plaza can get pretty busy, especially during major events like Indian Market or during the holidays. If you want to avoid the busiest times, try visiting during weekdays, or go early in the morning. That way, you can enjoy the Plaza without feeling overwhelmed by crowds.

What makes the Historic Santa Fe Plaza stand out, compared to other city squares or similar places in the U.S., is its combination of rich history, cultural significance, and artistic flair. You'll find influences from the Spanish, Native American, and Anglo cultures all coming together in a way that's uniquely Santa Fe. The Plaza feels like a living testament to the city's diversity and history. For me, it's more than just a place to shop or eat – it's the very essence of Santa Fe, and a perfect introduction to the city.

Whether you're visiting for a day or staying for longer, the Plaza will undoubtedly be one of the highlights of your time in Santa Fe. It's a place that you can explore at your own pace, whether you're admiring the architecture, enjoying the local food, or simply taking in the beauty of the surroundings. Every time I visit, there's something new to discover.

Loretto Chapel and the Miraculous Staircase

Loretto Chapel, located at 207 Old Santa Fe Trail, is one of Santa Fe's most captivating landmarks. The moment you step inside, you're greeted by the sense of quiet reverence, and the soft, golden light that filters through the stained-glass windows gives the chapel an almost ethereal glow. As soon as I arrived, I could tell this place had a story to tell. The chapel itself is beautiful with its gothic architecture, but what really sets it apart is its famous Miraculous Staircase.

Getting there was a breeze for me, as it's centrally located in the heart of Santa Fe, just a short walk from the Historic Santa Fe Plaza. If you're coming from the Plaza, it's only about a 10-minute stroll. If you're driving, there's parking available nearby, but it can get busy during peak times, so it's best to arrive early if you can. The chapel is open daily, and while there's an entrance fee, it's well worth it. As of now, the fee is

$5 for adults, with discounts for seniors and children. It's a small price to pay for the experience you'll have here.

When you first walk into Loretto Chapel, it's easy to get lost in the grandeur of the architecture—the soaring ceilings, the intricately carved woodwork, and the peaceful ambiance that fills the space. But the highlight, of course, is the Miraculous Staircase. This spiral staircase is the stuff of legend, and it's impossible not to be mesmerized by its beauty and craftsmanship. The staircase, with its seemingly gravity-defying design, has no visible means of support. It's a true engineering marvel, and the story behind it makes it even more fascinating.

According to the legend, the nuns who once lived in the chapel were in desperate need of a way to reach the choir loft, as the only staircase in the chapel was too steep and narrow. After praying for a solution, a mysterious carpenter appeared and built the staircase in just a few months. He used no nails, only wooden pegs, and when he finished, he disappeared as mysteriously as he had arrived, leaving behind a staircase that has continued to defy logic and explanation for over a century.

As I stood there, gazing up at the staircase, I couldn't help but marvel at the craftsmanship. It was even more beautiful in person than I had imagined from photos. The delicate curves and the way the steps seem to float without any visible support is something you truly have to see to believe. Visitors are allowed to walk around the base of the staircase, and there's a small area where you can get a closer look, but the staircase itself is roped off to preserve its integrity.

To make the most of your time at Loretto Chapel, take your time to absorb the beauty of the chapel itself. The stained glass windows are incredible, and the soft lighting creates a peaceful atmosphere that's perfect for reflection. I recommend sitting for a while, just listening to the stillness, and letting the beauty of the space sink in. There's also a gift shop in the chapel where you can purchase religious and spiritual items, including copies of the staircase, which makes for a perfect souvenir.

For those who are interested in history or architecture, Loretto Chapel is a must-see. It's not just about the staircase, but about the history that surrounds it. The chapel itself was built in the late 1800s and was originally part of a larger convent. It's now a place of pilgrimage and a reminder of Santa Fe's rich religious and cultural history.

In terms of crowd management, Loretto Chapel can get busy, especially on weekends and during tourist season. To avoid the crowds, I suggest visiting early in the morning, just after the chapel opens, or later in the afternoon. This way, you can enjoy the space without the distraction of too many people. The chapel is relatively small, so it can feel crowded quickly, but with a little patience, you can have a peaceful experience.

Overall, Loretto Chapel and the Miraculous Staircase are a unique part of Santa Fe that should be on every visitor's itinerary. Whether you're religious or simply in awe of craftsmanship, this is a place that offers something special. For me, it was a moment of serenity and wonder, a chance to experience a piece of Santa Fe's history and culture that continues to inspire people from all walks of life.

The Cathedral Basilica of St. Francis of Assisi

The Cathedral Basilica of St. Francis of Assisi is one of Santa Fe's most treasured landmarks, a stunning architectural masterpiece that reflects the city's rich history and deep spiritual roots. Located at 131 Cathedral Place, Santa Fe, New Mexico, this iconic cathedral is easily accessible, situated just a short walk from the heart of the historic Santa Fe Plaza. Its towering spires and Romanesque Revival design stand in striking contrast to the surrounding adobe structures, making it a beacon for visitors exploring the city.

Getting to the cathedral is straightforward. If you're staying near the Plaza, you can easily reach it on foot, enjoying the charm of Santa Fe's pedestrian-friendly streets along the way. For those arriving by car, there are several parking options nearby, including public parking garages and street parking.

Local bus services also connect to the area, with stops within a few blocks of the cathedral.

Entrance to the Cathedral Basilica of St. Francis of Assisi is free, welcoming all who wish to admire its beauty or seek a moment of reflection. The cathedral's doors are open most days from morning until late afternoon, but it's always a good idea to check the schedule if you plan to attend a specific event or mass.

As you step inside, you'll be immediately captivated by the serene and majestic atmosphere. The high vaulted ceilings, intricate stained-glass windows imported from France, and beautiful stonework create a sense of reverence and wonder. One of the highlights of the interior is the statue of Our Lady of Peace, a cherished symbol of faith and devotion. The statue, originally brought to Santa Fe in 1626, is the oldest representation of the Virgin Mary in the United States and holds a significant place in the hearts of locals.

Take your time exploring the cathedral's many artistic and architectural details. The intricate wood carvings, decorative frescoes, and the impressive altar are worth close inspection. The Stations of the Cross, meticulously rendered, invite quiet contemplation as you walk along them. Whether you're interested in history, art, or spirituality, the cathedral offers a deeply enriching experience.

Outside, the cathedral grounds are equally enchanting. The peaceful courtyard is adorned with statues and a beautiful rose garden, which is particularly lovely in the warmer months.

One statue not to miss is the bronze depiction of St. Francis of Assisi, the patron saint of the cathedral, often surrounded by pigeons and other birds that seem to sense the saint's connection to nature.

To fully enjoy your visit, consider timing your stop to coincide with one of the cathedral's musical performances or special services, which showcase the exceptional acoustics of the space and the talent of local choirs and musicians. If you're visiting during the Christmas season, the luminarias and holiday decorations create an especially magical atmosphere.

Before you leave, take a moment to step back and admire the cathedral from the outside. The main façade, with its intricate carvings and symmetrical design, is a sight to behold. This is a perfect spot for photos, particularly in the soft light of early morning or late afternoon when the stone takes on a warm, golden hue.

Nearby, you'll find plenty of places to grab a coffee or a meal if you want to extend your exploration of the area. Santa Fe's vibrant downtown offers a blend of modern and traditional eateries, art galleries, and shops, making it easy to pair your visit to the cathedral with other activities.

The Cathedral Basilica of St. Francis of Assisi is not just a place of worship; it's a testament to Santa Fe's enduring cultural and spiritual heritage. Whether you come to pray, to admire its beauty, or simply to soak in the peaceful ambiance, your time here is sure to leave a lasting impression.

Meow Wolf: An Immersive Art Adventure

Meow Wolf in Santa Fe is an experience unlike any other, a wildly imaginative, interactive art installation that transcends the boundaries of traditional galleries and museums. Located at 1352 Rufina Circle, Santa Fe, New Mexico, it's a must-visit for anyone seeking a blend of creativity, mystery, and playful exploration. Known as the House of Eternal Return, Meow Wolf invites visitors into an otherworldly adventure through its immersive storytelling and mind-bending visuals.

Reaching Meow Wolf is convenient. If you're driving, it's just a short distance from downtown Santa Fe, taking about 10-15 minutes. Parking is available on-site, and it's free, so you won't need to worry about finding a spot. For those using public transportation, the Santa Fe Trails bus system has routes that stop nearby, making it accessible even without a car.

Alternatively, ride-share services like Uber or Lyft are reliable and easy to use in Santa Fe.

Entrance to Meow Wolf is ticketed, with prices varying depending on age and residency. General admission for adults is usually around $50, with discounted rates for children, seniors, and New Mexico residents. It's best to purchase tickets in advance through their website, as this popular attraction can sell out, especially on weekends and during holidays. The experience is worth every penny, offering hours of entertainment and discovery.

Once inside, prepare to leave reality behind. The story begins in what appears to be a normal house, but you'll quickly notice that not everything is as it seems. Doors open into secret passages, refrigerators lead to glowing tunnels, and wardrobes transport you to alternate dimensions. The House of Eternal Return is built around the concept of a mysterious disappearance, and as you wander through the various rooms and spaces, you can piece together clues about the enigmatic family and the strange phenomena that surround them.

To fully enjoy your time, let your curiosity guide you. Touch everything, open every door, and don't hesitate to crawl through tight spaces or climb up hidden staircases. Each room is a masterpiece of creativity, featuring works from local and international artists. From neon-lit forests to surreal dreamscapes, the environments are as diverse as they are stunning. The space is designed to be interactive, so take your time to play with the installations, listen to sounds, and discover the many layers of the story.

For families, Meow Wolf is a fantastic destination. Children will love the vibrant colors, playful designs, and countless opportunities to explore. Adults, too, will find themselves captivated by the intricate details and deeper narratives woven throughout the exhibit. It's an experience that bridges generations, offering something for everyone.

Make sure to wear comfortable shoes, as you'll be on your feet for a good portion of your visit. Plan for at least two to three hours to fully explore the space, though many visitors find themselves staying even longer as they get lost in the world of Meow Wolf. If you need a break, there's a café on-site where you can grab a snack or a drink before diving back into the adventure.

Don't forget to check out the gift shop on your way out. It's filled with unique merchandise, from quirky souvenirs to artist-designed items that make perfect mementos of your visit. You might also find information about special events, as Meow Wolf often hosts concerts, workshops, and themed nights that add an extra layer of excitement to the experience.

Meow Wolf is more than just an art installation; it's a journey into the imagination, a place where creativity knows no bounds. Whether you're an art lover, a family looking for fun, or someone simply curious about this much-talked-about destination, the House of Eternal Return promises a day of awe and inspiration. It's a Santa Fe treasure that will leave you thinking about the possibilities of art and storytelling long after you leave.

The New Mexico State Capitol

The New Mexico State Capitol, located at 490 Old Santa Fe Trail, Santa Fe, New Mexico, is a fascinating blend of history, culture, and government. Known as the Roundhouse due to its unique circular design, this building stands out not only as the seat of the state legislature but also as a significant architectural and artistic landmark. It is a place where New Mexico's past and present come together, offering visitors an insightful and enriching experience.

Getting to the New Mexico State Capitol is quite easy. If you're driving, the Capitol is centrally located, just a few blocks south of the Santa Fe Plaza, with ample free parking available in nearby lots. Public transportation, such as the Santa Fe Trails bus system, also has stops close to the Capitol, making it accessible even if you don't have a car. For those who enjoy walking, the Capitol is within a reasonable distance from many downtown attractions and hotels, making it a pleasant stroll through Santa Fe's charming streets.

One of the most appealing aspects of the New Mexico State Capitol is that it is free to visit. Open to the public year-round during weekdays, this building invites both locals and tourists to explore its halls and learn more about the state's governance, history, and artistic heritage. Guided tours are available, but self-guided exploration is just as rewarding, allowing you to take in the spaces at your own pace.

As you approach the building, its striking architecture immediately catches your attention. Completed in 1966, the Roundhouse is the only circular state capitol in the United States, symbolizing unity and inclusivity. The design reflects elements of New Mexico's Native American, Hispanic, and Anglo cultures, with traditional motifs and a sense of harmony with the surrounding landscape.

Inside, you'll find a treasure trove of art and history. The Capitol Art Collection is a highlight, featuring over 600 works by New Mexican artists. Paintings, sculptures, photographs, and mixed-media pieces line the walls and spaces, showcasing the state's rich cultural diversity and creative spirit. Be sure to admire the stunning rotunda, where the circular skylight bathes the space in natural light, creating a serene and inspiring atmosphere.

Take some time to visit the legislative chambers, which are open to visitors when not in session. These spaces are not only functional but also beautifully designed, with details that reflect New Mexico's unique heritage. If your visit coincides with the legislative session, you might even have the opportunity to observe proceedings, gaining insight into the workings of state government.

For a deeper understanding of the Capitol's art and architecture, consider joining a free guided tour. These tours provide valuable context, explaining the significance of the artwork, the symbolism behind the building's design, and the role of the legislature. Knowledgeable guides bring the history and stories of the Roundhouse to life, making the experience even more engaging.

To make the most of your visit, allow at least an hour to explore the building. Wear comfortable shoes, as there is quite a bit of walking involved, especially if you choose to explore the surrounding grounds. Outside the Capitol, you'll find beautifully landscaped gardens and sculptures, offering a tranquil space to relax and reflect.

The New Mexico State Capitol is not just a place for politics; it's a celebration of the state's identity, blending governance with culture and art in a way that few other capitols do. Whether you're a history enthusiast, an art lover, or simply curious about New Mexico's heritage, a visit to the Roundhouse is sure to leave a lasting impression. It's an experience that combines education, inspiration, and a deep appreciation for the unique spirit of New Mexico.

CHAPTER 7.
OUTDOOR ADVENTURES
Hiking Trails

Santa Fe is surrounded by stunning natural beauty, and one of the best ways to experience it is by hiking the trails in and around the Santa Fe National Forest. The forest is located just outside the city, and it's filled with trails for all levels, whether you're looking for a leisurely stroll or an adventurous trek through the mountains. Getting there is easy—just a short drive from downtown Santa Fe, and the forest is easily accessible via Highway 475, which leads you right into the heart of the forest.

The Santa Fe National Forest itself spans over 1.5 million acres, offering a vast range of landscapes from deep forests to alpine meadows and stunning mountain vistas. I was excited for the chance to explore the trails, and I decided to start with one of the more popular routes, the Windsor Trail. The trailhead is located off Highway 475, and you'll find a small parking area where you can leave your car before beginning the hike. The Windsor Trail is about 10 miles long and offers a moderate challenge, which was perfect for my energy level. The beauty of this trail is that it takes you through diverse landscapes, from shady forests to open meadows with beautiful views of the surrounding mountains.

The thing I loved most about the Windsor Trail was how quiet it felt. Even though I wasn't too far from the city, the sounds of the forest took over—birds calling, the rustling of leaves, and the sound of a nearby creek running gently. It was peaceful, and I could feel myself disconnecting from the bustle of daily life. As I walked, I noticed the wildflowers starting to bloom in the spring sun, adding bursts of color along the trail. The hike wasn't too difficult, but there were a few spots with some incline that required a little more effort. However, the beauty of the surroundings kept me motivated, and there were plenty of spots to stop and take in the views.

Another trail I highly recommend is the Atalaya Mountain Trail, which starts from the Atalaya Trailhead on the east side of the city. This trail is a bit shorter—only about 4 miles—but it offers some of the best panoramic views of Santa Fe. The hike up Atalaya Mountain is steeper than the Windsor Trail, but the views from the top are absolutely worth it. From the summit, you can see all of Santa Fe spread out below, with the Jemez Mountains in the distance. On clear days, the vistas are breathtaking, and I found myself spending a while up there just soaking in the beauty of the city and surrounding wilderness.

If you're looking for something a bit more remote, the Pecos Wilderness is a great choice. Located a little farther out from the Santa Fe city center, it offers more challenging hikes, with higher elevations and more rugged terrain. I took a drive out to the trailhead of the Winsor Trail, which starts in the Pecos Wilderness, and it was a bit of a longer drive, but the landscape more than made up for it. This area is perfect for those who want to escape into the wilderness and experience a more secluded part of New Mexico's natural beauty. The Pecos Wilderness has stunning alpine lakes and tall, dense forests, and the trails here can take you deep into the mountains for a truly immersive experience.

The great thing about hiking in the Santa Fe area is that there's something for everyone. Whether you're a seasoned hiker or just looking for a short walk, there are trails of all levels. I also found that many of the trails are well-marked, which made navigation easy. For anyone new to hiking or unfamiliar with the area, I would recommend stopping at a local visitor center to pick up a map of the trails. There's a visitor center at the Santa Fe National Forest headquarters located at 11 Forest Lane. The staff there is super friendly and helpful, and they can recommend specific trails based on your experience level or what you're looking for.

If you're planning to go hiking in Santa Fe, there are a few tips that will help you get the most out of your experience. First, always bring plenty of water, especially if you're hiking in the warmer months. The sun can be intense, even at higher elevations, and staying hydrated is key. It's also a good idea to wear sturdy shoes with good traction, as some of the trails can be rocky and uneven. I also recommend bringing sunscreen and a hat, since the sun is strong at higher altitudes, even if the temperature feels cooler.

One of the best things about hiking in Santa Fe is that you can enjoy the outdoors year-round. In the spring and summer, the trails are lush and green, with wildflowers in bloom and plenty of wildlife to spot. Fall is another amazing time to visit, as the foliage turns vibrant shades of red, orange, and gold, creating a beautiful backdrop for any hike. Even in winter, there are still plenty of opportunities for snowshoeing or cross-country skiing if you're up for a snowy adventure.

In terms of costs, most of the trails in the Santa Fe National Forest are free to access, which is a huge bonus. However, if you're parking in certain areas or using specific trailheads, there may be a small fee for parking, typically around $5. It's also worth noting that if you plan to camp or spend an extended period in the wilderness, you may need a permit, so be sure to check ahead.

When it comes to crowd management, Santa Fe's trails can get busy, especially during peak tourist seasons like summer, so I suggest going early in the morning if you want a more peaceful experience. Many of the trails are also accessible on weekdays, which can make it easier to avoid large crowds.

Ski Santa Fe: Winter Sports and Year-Round Views

Ski Santa Fe is a fantastic place to enjoy winter sports, but it's also a year-round destination with breathtaking views, making it an ideal spot for both adventure and relaxation. Located about 16 miles from the heart of Santa Fe, the ski area is easy to reach by car, and it's a beautiful drive up into the mountains. The address is 100 Sunrise Drive, Santa Fe, NM 87501, and the road leading there, NM-475, takes you up through the stunning Sangre de Cristo Mountains. The drive itself is an experience, with winding roads, tall pines, and views of the surrounding valleys.

If you're planning to visit during the winter months, Ski Santa Fe is a wonderful place to enjoy skiing and snowboarding. The slopes here are known for being less crowded than some of the bigger ski resorts, which means you can enjoy more runs and a more relaxed atmosphere. When I arrived, I was immediately struck by how welcoming the place felt. The staff at the base area are friendly and ready to help, whether you're renting equipment or getting your lift ticket. If you're new to skiing, there are great beginner areas, and the instructors are experienced, making it easy to get started.

The resort offers a variety of slopes, ranging from easy to expert, so there's something for everyone, whether you're just learning or looking to challenge yourself. I personally enjoyed the intermediate runs, where the snow was soft and the views were amazing. From almost every part of the mountain, you can see the beautiful landscapes surrounding Santa Fe. The views of the mountains and valleys are just stunning, especially as the sun rises and bathes everything in golden light. If you're not skiing, the scenic chairlift rides are a great way to enjoy the views and take some pictures.

Ski Santa Fe is not just for skiers and snowboarders. Even if you don't hit the slopes, there's plenty to do here. The resort has snowshoeing trails and even a small snow tubing area, which is a fun way to spend time with family or friends. In addition to the snow activities, there are cozy places to warm up inside. The lodge at the base of the mountain offers a great place to relax, grab a hot drink, or enjoy a meal while taking in the views.

The best part about Ski Santa Fe is that it's a great place to visit any time of year. During the warmer months, the area transforms into a hiking paradise, and you'll find plenty of trails that lead you through the forest and up to higher elevations. The terrain changes dramatically from winter to summer, but the beauty of the place remains constant. One of my favorite things to do in the summer was to hike up from the base area and take in the cool mountain air and the incredible views of Santa Fe below. The summer months are less crowded, and hiking offers an escape into nature with quiet, peaceful trails.

If you're looking to visit, I'd recommend checking the Ski Santa Fe website ahead of time to get the most up-to-date information on trail conditions or lift hours, especially if you're planning to visit during the busy winter season. While skiing and snowboarding are the main draws in winter, I've always found the resort to be a place of great peace and beauty no matter the time of year.

Getting there is easy, but be aware that the road leading up to the resort can be narrow and winding, so it's important to drive cautiously. In winter, snow tires or chains may be required, especially after a fresh snowfall. Parking at the resort is convenient, and there are plenty of spaces available even on busy days, although I suggest arriving early to get the best spots close to the lodge.

For anyone visiting Ski Santa Fe, the cost can vary depending on the time of year. Lift tickets for skiing or snowboarding can be purchased in advance, which may save you a little bit of money. Rental equipment is available, and there's a ski school if you need a lesson. For those not skiing, taking a scenic chairlift ride or just exploring the area by foot is completely free, and it's a wonderful way to enjoy the surroundings without the expense of skiing or snowboarding.

Overall, Ski Santa Fe offers something for everyone. Whether you're an avid skier or snowboarder, someone who enjoys peaceful mountain hikes, or just looking to experience stunning views, this is a place to visit. The mountain's natural beauty, combined with the variety of activities available, makes it a must-see destination for anyone in Santa Fe. Even if you're not into winter sports, the mountain's year-round charm is enough to make a trip worth it.

Rafting and Water Activities along the Rio Grande

Rafting and water activities along the Rio Grande offer an unforgettable way to experience the rugged beauty and natural splendor of New Mexico. Stretching across diverse landscapes, this iconic river winds through breathtaking canyons, serene valleys, and untamed wilderness, making it a perfect setting for outdoor adventure and connection with nature.

The Rio Grande is easily accessible from Santa Fe, with several rafting companies and activity hubs located in and around the nearby town of Pilar, approximately 45 minutes to an hour's drive north of Santa Fe. Following US-84/285 towards Española and then taking NM-68 through the picturesque Rio Grande Gorge will lead you to the heart of the action. Look for well-known outfitters such as Far Flung Adventures, located at

15 NM-522 in El Prado, and New Mexico River Adventures at 2217 NM-68 in Embudo. These locations serve as starting points for many guided trips.

Rafting the Rio Grande typically involves organized tours, which are paid experiences. Prices vary depending on the type of trip you choose, ranging from tranquil family-friendly floats to adrenaline-pumping whitewater adventures through the thrilling Class III rapids of the Taos Box. Outfitters usually provide all necessary gear, including life jackets, helmets, and paddles, ensuring a safe and enjoyable outing. Some trips also include transportation from Santa Fe or meeting points along the river.

Beginner-friendly routes, like the Orilla Verde section near Pilar, are ideal for those new to rafting or seeking a relaxing journey. This stretch meanders through calm waters, offering incredible views of the surrounding high desert landscape and opportunities to spot wildlife such as great blue herons, mule deer, and even bald eagles. Guides often share stories about the geology, history, and cultural significance of the Rio Grande, enriching the experience beyond the water.

For thrill-seekers, the Taos Box section of the river is a must. This 16-mile stretch of rapids demands teamwork and concentration, rewarding adventurers with an exhilarating ride through narrow gorges and dramatic rock formations. The spring runoff season, usually from May to early July, provides the most exciting conditions, as snowmelt from the Sangre de Cristo Mountains swells the river.

Beyond rafting, the Rio Grande offers a range of other water activities. Kayaking and paddleboarding are popular for those who want a more individual challenge. Equipment rentals and lessons are available from many outfitters, catering to all skill levels. The calm waters of the Orilla Verde or the Rio Grande del Norte National Monument are perfect for leisurely paddling while taking in the striking scenery.

Fishing enthusiasts will also find the Rio Grande a haven. The river is home to a variety of fish species, including brown and rainbow trout. Guided fishing trips can be arranged, or you can venture out on your own. Ensure you have a valid New Mexico fishing license, which can be obtained online or at local sporting goods stores.

For those who prefer to enjoy the river without getting wet, the area around the Rio Grande Gorge Bridge, just outside Taos, offers incredible hiking trails and vantage points. The bridge itself, spanning 600 feet above the river, provides breathtaking views of the gorge and is a great spot for photos.

To make the most of your time along the Rio Grande, come prepared with essentials such as sunscreen, a hat, sturdy water shoes, and plenty of water to stay hydrated. Guided trips often provide snacks or meals, but it's always a good idea to bring your own in case you spend additional time exploring the area.

Rafting and water activities along the Rio Grande are more than just adventures; they are an opportunity to immerse yourself in the natural beauty of northern New Mexico, connect with its vibrant ecosystem, and create memories that will last a lifetime. Whether you're navigating roaring rapids, gliding through calm waters, or simply marveling at the sheer cliffs of the gorge, the Rio Grande promises an experience that is as exhilarating as it is serene.

Exploring Bandelier National Monument and Kasha-Katuwe Tent Rocks

Exploring Bandelier National Monument and Kasha-Katuwe Tent Rocks is an unforgettable experience that takes you deep into New Mexico's history and natural beauty. These two sites are perfect for anyone who loves outdoor adventures, stunning landscapes, and discovering ancient cultures.

Bandelier National Monument, located at 15 Entrance Rd, Los Alamos, NM 87544, is a treasure trove of history and natural wonders. To get there from Santa Fe, you'll need to drive about 45 minutes northwest. The road takes you through scenic areas, and as you approach the park, you can already feel the change in the landscape. The monument is open year-round, and there's no entrance fee, though donations are always appreciated. Once you arrive, I recommend stopping by the visitor center first. It's a great place to get maps, learn about the park's history, and pick up some helpful advice on the best trails and sites to visit.

One of the most striking features of Bandelier is its ancient cliff dwellings. These are the homes of the Ancestral Puebloans, who lived in the area more than 600 years ago. The famous Frijoles Canyon is where you'll find these dwellings, and you can explore them via the Main Loop Trail. The hike is easy to moderate, about 1.2 miles, and it takes you past the cliffside homes, some of which you can actually climb into. As I walked along the trail, I couldn't help but feel amazed by how the Puebloans built their homes into the cliffs. It's a powerful reminder of the ingenuity and resilience of the people who once lived here.

Along the Main Loop Trail, you'll also encounter petroglyphs and remnants of ancient structures. It's a very peaceful place, and the views of the canyon are breathtaking, with the green landscape contrasting against the red sandstone cliffs. If you want to take your experience to the next level, there's also the longer Alcove House Trail. This 1.5-mile trail is a bit more strenuous but offers a climb up a ladder to reach a large cave dwelling high in the cliffs. The panoramic view from the top is incredible, and you'll have a sense of what it must have been like to live in this remote area so long ago.

After Bandelier, head to Kasha-Katuwe Tent Rocks National Monument, which is located at 8 D Wells Rd, Cochiti Pueblo, NM 87072. From Santa Fe, it's about a 45-minute drive south, and once again, the journey offers some beautiful desert views along the way. The entrance fee is $25 per vehicle, which is well worth it for the stunning views and unique rock formations you'll see. Kasha-Katuwe Tent Rocks is named for its unique rock formations that look like large, ancient tents. These formations were created over millions of years from volcanic eruptions and the subsequent erosion of softer layers of rock. It's one of those places that feels almost otherworldly.

The main trail at Tent Rocks is a 1.5-mile loop that takes you through narrow slot canyons, past towering rock spires, and up to a viewpoint that offers panoramic views of the surrounding desert and the Sandia Mountains in the distance. As I walked through the slot canyons, I was struck by how narrow and winding they were. The rock walls seem to rise up on either side, and the sunlight filtering through creates a magical atmosphere. The hike is moderate, with some steep sections, but the trail is well-maintained and definitely doable for most people. Once you reach the top, you'll be rewarded with a breathtaking view of the cone-shaped tent rocks stretching out below.

What makes Kasha-Katuwe Tent Rocks so special is not just the scenery but the sense of peace and solitude you feel while hiking. It's a quiet, almost meditative experience as you explore the canyon and marvel at the towering spires around you. There's also a variety of wildlife to be seen, including lizards, birds, and desert plants, which make the hike even more enjoyable.

To get the most out of your visit to both Bandelier and Tent Rocks, it's a good idea to bring plenty of water, especially during the warmer months. Wear sturdy hiking shoes, as the trails can be rocky and uneven in places. I also recommend bringing sunscreen and a hat, as the sun can be intense at both sites, especially in the summer. If you visit during the spring or fall, the temperatures are more moderate, making for a more comfortable hiking experience.

Both Bandelier and Kasha-Katuwe Tent Rocks offer a combination of natural beauty, outdoor exploration, and historical significance. The cliff dwellings at Bandelier are a reminder of the rich cultural heritage of the Puebloan people, while the rock formations at Tent Rocks feel like something out of a dream, offering a chance to connect with the land in a deep and meaningful way.

One of the best things about visiting these sites is that they are not overly crowded, especially if you go early in the morning or later in the afternoon. This allows you to experience the peacefulness of the surroundings and really take your time to explore. For those interested in local history and culture, both Bandelier and Tent Rocks provide a fascinating glimpse into New Mexico's past and its unique geological features.

Both places offer a wonderful balance of hiking, history, and natural beauty, making them must-visit destinations for anyone coming to Santa Fe. The landscapes, the quiet moments, and the connection to ancient history are experiences that stay with you long after your visit.

CHAPTER 8.
FOOD AND DRINK

The Flavors of New Mexican Cuisine

Exploring the unique flavors of New Mexican cuisine is like embarking on a sensory journey that reflects the region's vibrant history, diverse cultural influences, and connection to the land. At its heart, New Mexican food is a celebration of bold, earthy, and dynamic flavors, shaped by indigenous, Spanish, and Mexican traditions. Five distinct flavors stand out in this culinary tradition, each offering a unique taste of the region's soul.

The first and perhaps most iconic flavor is the New Mexico chile. Available in red, green, or the famed Christmas-style blend of both, these chiles are the cornerstone of New Mexican cuisine. Green chiles are picked fresh and roasted, imparting a smoky, slightly tangy heat that transforms everything from enchiladas to cheeseburgers. Red chiles, ripened and dried, develop a deeper, earthier sweetness that's often turned into rich sauces. Whether draped over huevos rancheros or stewed into posole, the chile's complexity is unrivaled. For those with spice sensitivities, many restaurants offer mild versions of these dishes or allow you to request the chile sauce on the side.

Next is blue corn, a staple ingredient rooted in the region's Native American heritage. Blue corn is more than just a visual delight with its striking color; it has a nutty, slightly sweet flavor that elevates tortillas, tamales, and pancakes. Rich in antioxidants and lower on the glycemic index compared to yellow corn, it's a nutritious option for many diners. Those with gluten sensitivities will be pleased to know that blue corn is naturally gluten-free, but it's wise to confirm with your server that no cross-contamination has occurred in preparation.

Another distinctive flavor comes from piñon nuts, the seeds of New Mexico's native pine trees. These buttery, slightly sweet nuts are a treasured ingredient in local sweets, such as biscochitos, or sprinkled over savory dishes for added texture. Piñon harvesting is an important cultural practice in the state, symbolizing a deep connection to the land. For visitors with nut allergies, it's important to ask if a dish contains piñon or if it has been prepared in proximity to them, as their inclusion can sometimes be subtle.

The tangy, fermented notes of red and green chile ristras—strings of dried chiles used for decoration and cooking—offer another unique layer of flavor. These are not merely ornamental; the drying process intensifies the chiles' natural sweetness and imparts a distinct smokiness. When cooked into sauces or salsas, these flavors become concentrated and deeply satisfying. If you're sensitive to acidic foods, it's a good idea to balance these flavors with a side of creamy guacamole or cheese, both of which are commonly served alongside chile-based dishes.

Finally, the smoky, herbal flavor of Mexican oregano is an essential seasoning in New Mexican cooking. Different from Mediterranean oregano, this variety has a more robust, citrusy character that enhances stews, meats, and salsas. It's often paired with cumin and garlic to create the rich, layered profiles typical of carne adovada or green chile stew. For individuals with sensitivities to spices, Mexican oregano can be omitted in some dishes without losing the overall depth of flavor, so don't hesitate to request adjustments when ordering.

For those with dietary restrictions, Santa Fe's vibrant culinary scene offers numerous options to enjoy these flavors safely. Many restaurants provide gluten-free, vegan, and vegetarian alternatives, and servers are well-versed in guiding guests through menu choices to accommodate allergies. Additionally, the use of fresh, local ingredients means that dishes can often be customized without sacrificing flavor.

To fully appreciate New Mexican cuisine, embrace the philosophy of slow eating and savoring. Take time to enjoy the balance of smoky, tangy, sweet, and earthy notes that define each dish. Whether you're indulging in a plate of blue corn enchiladas smothered in green chile, nibbling on piñon-studded cookies, or sipping on a margarita infused with local herbs, the flavors of New Mexico are as unforgettable as its landscapes.

Iconic Restaurants and Local Favorites

Santa Fe is a culinary paradise, where the flavors of New Mexican cuisine blend with creative, contemporary dishes. Whether you're seeking an upscale dining experience or a casual local eatery, Santa Fe offers a variety of dining options to suit every taste and budget. Here are some must-try spots to explore:

1. The Shed
- Atmosphere: The Shed offers a cozy, traditional New Mexican ambiance, with its adobe walls and wooden tables. It has a casual, family-friendly atmosphere, perfect for a relaxed meal with a bit of local charm. The restaurant is often bustling with locals and visitors alike, which only adds to its lively, welcoming vibe.
- Pricing: Moderate. Appetizers typically cost between $6–$10, while main courses like enchiladas or chile rellenos are priced around $15–$25. Desserts, including sopapillas, are usually around $6.
- Signature Dishes: The red and green chile enchiladas are a must-try, served with rich, flavorful sauces that showcase the essence of New Mexico's chile peppers. Also, the green chile stew is a hearty, comforting dish with tender pork and potatoes in a flavorful broth.

2. Café Pasqual's
- Atmosphere: Café Pasqual's has a lively, eclectic atmosphere with vibrant decor, local art, and a cozy, intimate feel. It's a great spot for breakfast or brunch, often filled with the hum of conversation and the scent of freshly prepared food. It's casual yet has a certain charm that makes it feel special.

- Pricing: Moderate to high. Breakfast or brunch options like huevos rancheros or a tamale plate range from $12–$20. For dinner, expect to spend around $20–$30 for most entrees, such as grilled salmon or carne adovada.
- Signature Dishes: The huevos rancheros are exceptional, made with farm-fresh eggs, crispy tortillas, and a perfectly balanced red or green chile sauce. Another standout is the carne adovada, a tender pork dish marinated in red chile, slow-cooked to perfection, and served with beans and rice.

3. Geronimo
- Atmosphere: Geronimo is a refined, upscale restaurant housed in a historic adobe home. The setting is elegant, with dim lighting, rustic wooden beams, and a romantic ambiance. This is the place to go for a special occasion or a sophisticated dining experience.
- Pricing: Expensive. Main courses generally range from $30–$50, while appetizers range from $12–$18. Desserts typically cost around $8–$12.
- Signature Dishes: Geronimo's elk tenderloin is a showstopper, served with rich sauces and perfectly cooked vegetables. The crab and lobster bisque is another favorite, velvety smooth and incredibly flavorful, offering a luxurious start to any meal. For dessert, the chocolate soufflé is divine, a perfect balance of rich chocolate and light texture.

4. Sazon
- Atmosphere: This intimate, upscale restaurant offers a modern take on traditional New Mexican cuisine, with a sleek and sophisticated atmosphere. The space is cozy, with

contemporary touches, and it's perfect for a romantic dinner or a special gathering.
- Pricing: On the higher end, with appetizers starting at around $10 and main courses typically priced between $20–$35. Desserts are around $7–$10.
- Signature Dishes: The duck enchiladas are a unique twist on the classic dish, combining the tender richness of duck with smoky chile sauces. The pork belly with mole is another standout, rich and flavorful, with a perfect balance of savory and sweet notes. Don't forget to try the saffron ice cream for dessert, a perfect ending to the meal.

5. The Cowgirl BBQ
- Atmosphere: The Cowgirl BBQ has a fun, laid-back atmosphere with a Western theme. The casual setting is perfect for families and groups, and there's often live music, adding to the vibrant vibe. It's a great spot to relax with some hearty food and a cold drink.
- Pricing: Affordable to moderate. Most main dishes are priced between $12–$20, with appetizers like fried pickles or BBQ sliders costing around $6–$10. Desserts like the chocolate pecan pie are around $5–$8.
- Signature Dishes: The BBQ ribs are a crowd favorite, tender and falling off the bone, with a smoky, flavorful glaze. The green chile cheeseburger is another popular choice, packed with flavor and topped with a generous helping of New Mexico's signature chile. The chocolate pecan pie is a must-try for dessert—rich, gooey, and the perfect end to a hearty meal.

6. Cafe Sf

- Atmosphere: Located inside the Hotel Santa Fe, Cafe Sf offers an elegant yet casual atmosphere, perfect for a relaxed lunch or dinner. The decor blends traditional Southwest elements with contemporary touches, creating a comfortable and stylish environment.
- Pricing: Moderate. Main dishes range from $15–$30, with lighter fare like salads and sandwiches costing around $10–$15. Desserts like the chocolate cake or cheesecake are priced at $6–$8.
- Signature Dishes: The chile-rubbed tuna is a standout, combining tender tuna with the distinctive heat of New Mexican chile. The buttermilk fried chicken is another popular option, crispy on the outside and juicy on the inside, served with seasonal sides.

7. Tomasita's
- Atmosphere: Tomasita's is a family-friendly, casual eatery that feels like a true Santa Fe institution. The colorful interior and warm, welcoming atmosphere make it a popular choice for both locals and visitors. It's perfect for a relaxed meal with great food and good company.
- Pricing: Affordable. Most dishes range from $10–$20, with combo plates or smaller portions available for around $12–$15. Desserts are priced between $5–$8.
- Signature Dishes: The red chile enchiladas and chile rellenos are among the most popular dishes, both showcasing the bold, smoky flavors that define New Mexican cuisine. The sopaipillas are a must-try dessert, warm and fluffy, served with honey for dipping.

8. La Choza

- Atmosphere: La Choza offers a cozy, casual setting that exudes authentic New Mexico charm. It's a family-owned spot with a relaxed vibe, making it perfect for those looking to enjoy a true taste of Santa Fe. The restaurant has colorful decor, local artwork, and a friendly, welcoming feel.
- Pricing: Moderate. Most entrees are priced between $12–$20, with combination plates available for around $15–$18. Desserts like the flan are around $6.
- Signature Dishes: The carne adovada is a must-try, a tender, slow-cooked pork dish with rich red chile sauce. The green chile cheeseburger is another local favorite, topped with plenty of flavorful chile.

Santa Fe's culinary scene is as rich and diverse as the city itself. Whether you're in the mood for traditional New Mexican fare, a sophisticated meal, or something casual with a twist, there's a spot that will make every meal memorable. Make sure to visit these local eateries for an authentic taste of Santa Fe's food culture.

Farmers' Markets and Food Festivals

Santa Fe is a city that celebrates its rich agricultural heritage, and one of the best ways to experience its local flavors is by visiting its farmers' markets and food festivals. These events offer a wonderful opportunity to explore the freshest produce, meet local farmers, and indulge in some of the most unique foods the region has to offer. Whether you're a foodie looking to sample new flavors or just enjoy the vibrant atmosphere, there's something special about shopping for local ingredients or attending a festival in Santa Fe.

The Santa Fe Farmers Market is one of the most popular and well-loved spots in the city. Located at 1607 Paseo de Peralta, this market is open year-round, with more vendors and a larger selection during the warmer months. It's a lively space filled with stalls offering fresh, organic produce, artisanal cheeses, baked goods, and handmade crafts. The market is a true community gathering place where you can chat with local farmers and artisans, hear about their sustainable farming practices, and even sample the products before buying. The vibrant energy of the market makes it a great place to spend a few hours, just strolling around, chatting with locals, and sampling fresh produce. Don't miss the fresh green chiles when they're in season – they're a staple of New Mexican cuisine and can be found at several stalls.

If you're visiting in the summer, the market also has live music, making it a fun, family-friendly atmosphere. You'll find everything from organic tomatoes, fresh herbs, and colorful peppers to homemade tortillas and locally roasted coffee. On Saturdays, the market is especially bustling, and it's the perfect place to pick up fresh ingredients for a picnic or even enjoy a light meal from one of the food vendors serving tacos, tamales, or empanadas.

Santa Fe also hosts several food festivals throughout the year, celebrating the city's love for local and regional cuisine. The Santa Fe Wine & Chile Fiesta, held every September, is one of the biggest events, attracting wine lovers and foodies alike. It's a week-long celebration of New Mexico's culinary offerings, where top chefs from around the country come together to showcase their skills. The highlight of the event is the Grand Tasting, where you can sample exquisite wines paired with signature dishes from local chefs. It's a great chance to try everything from roasted lamb and chile-laden enchiladas to decadent desserts. The festival is a wonderful blend of fine dining, community spirit, and a chance to savor some of the best flavors of Santa Fe.

Another popular event is the New Mexico Farmers' Market Association Annual Food and Farm Expo. Held in the fall, this festival focuses on the state's agricultural heritage, with cooking demonstrations, food tastings, and plenty of chances to shop from local vendors. You'll find everything from fresh produce and herbs to locally made jams, salsas, and even honey. It's a great opportunity to learn about sustainable farming practices and discover the unique flavors of New Mexico.

For something a little more seasonal, the Santa Fe Harvest Festival in October is a fun and family friendly event. It's a time when local farmers and producers gather to celebrate the bounty of the fall harvest, with pumpkin carving contests, live music, and a great selection of food to try. You can sample local produce, including apples, squash, and root vegetables, and enjoy everything from homemade pies to roasted corn. It's a festive and relaxed event, perfect for those who want to experience the flavors of the season.

Visiting these markets and festivals in Santa Fe offers more than just a chance to enjoy delicious food; it's a way to experience the local culture, meet the people who grow and prepare the food, and understand the importance of sustainability and local farming in New Mexico. Whether you're stocking up on fresh ingredients at the farmers' market or attending one of the city's lively food festivals, you'll leave with a deeper appreciation for the flavors and people of Santa Fe.

Breweries, Wineries, and Distilleries

Santa Fe is a city known for its vibrant arts scene and rich culinary traditions, but it also has a growing reputation for its craft beverages. Whether you're a beer enthusiast, a wine connoisseur, or a fan of handcrafted spirits, the local breweries, wineries, and distilleries offer something for everyone. Each stop provides a unique glimpse into Santa Fe's spirit of innovation and its deep connection to the land.

The local breweries in Santa Fe are a true testament to the city's creativity and dedication to producing high-quality, flavorful beers. One of the most well-known spots is Santa Fe Brewing Company, located at 37 Fireplace Rd. This brewery has been serving the city for over 30 years and is famous for its signature beers like the Happy Camper IPA and the State Pen Porter. The brewery's taproom is cozy and welcoming, with a laid-back vibe that invites you to relax and enjoy a cold pint. There's often live music and food trucks outside, making it a great place to spend an afternoon. The brewery also has a lovely beer garden where you can enjoy your drink while soaking in the beautiful Santa Fe weather. It's a must-visit for anyone who appreciates a well-crafted beer.

Another great stop for craft beer is the Rowley Farmhouse Ales, located at 3810 Old Pecos Trail. This place is a little different from the typical brewery. Rowley specializes in farmhouse ales, a style of beer that's brewed with local grains and often uses wild yeasts to give the beer a unique flavor. The brewery's tasting room has a rustic charm, with a warm, inviting atmosphere that feels like home. If you're looking to try something special, I highly recommend their Saison or the

Blonde Ale, both of which showcase their innovative approach to brewing.

Santa Fe's wineries are also an integral part of the local beverage scene. New Mexico's wine industry is one of the oldest in the United States, and the Santa Fe area boasts several excellent wineries. One of the standout wineries is the Estrella Del Norte Vineyard & Winery, located just outside of the city at 1111 Seneca Rd. The family-owned winery produces a range of wines, from reds to whites, and even a few sparkling varieties. The atmosphere here is relaxed, with beautiful vineyard views that make it a perfect spot for a wine tasting. The staff is knowledgeable and passionate about their craft, and they'll guide you through their selection of wines. I recommend trying their Riesling, which has a crisp, refreshing taste, or the Malbec, a smooth red with rich flavors.

For those who prefer a more intimate, boutique wine experience, the La Chiripada Winery is a hidden gem. Located at 920 W. Frontage Rd in Dixon, this small but charming winery offers personalized tastings and a selection of wines that reflect the region's unique terroir. The owners are passionate about sustainable farming practices, and the wines are made from grapes grown right on the property. The tasting room has a cozy, inviting atmosphere, and the wine flows generously. I particularly enjoyed their Tempranillo, which was smooth and flavorful, perfect for sipping while watching the sunset.

If spirits are more your style, Santa Fe has a growing distillery scene that's worth exploring. The Santa Fe Spirits Distillery is one of the most popular spots in the city, located at 308 Read St. This distillery is known for its high-quality, small-batch spirits, including vodka, gin, and whiskey. The tasting room has a modern, sleek design with a welcoming atmosphere. The staff is incredibly friendly and eager to share their knowledge about the distilling process. Don't miss their flagship Wheeler's Gin, which is infused with juniper and local herbs, giving it a distinct flavor that's perfect for cocktails. The Santa Fe Spirits Distillery also offers guided tours, where you can learn about the distilling process and sample some of their unique creations.

Another great place to try local spirits is the Colkegan Distillery, located at 1327 Siler Rd. Colkegan is known for its craft whiskey, which is made with mesquite wood for a smoky, distinctive flavor. The distillery's tasting room is rustic and comfortable, with knowledgeable staff who can guide you through a tasting. I highly recommend their Mesquite-Smoked Single Malt Whiskey, which has a smooth, smoky taste that's perfect for sipping neat or in a cocktail.

Santa Fe's breweries, wineries, and distilleries provide a wonderful opportunity to taste the local flavors and learn about the craftsmanship behind each beverage. Whether you're enjoying a cold beer on a sunny afternoon, sipping a glass of wine while overlooking the vineyards, or trying a locally-made spirit, these spots offer an unforgettable experience. Each stop has its own unique atmosphere, and all provide a chance to savor the creativity and passion that define Santa Fe's drink scene.

CHAPTER 9.
DAY TRIP AND EXCURSION

Taos and the High Road to Taos

Taos is a charming town nestled in northern New Mexico, surrounded by stunning natural beauty. It's known for its rich history, vibrant arts scene, and outdoor activities that draw visitors from all over the world. Getting to Taos is part of the adventure, especially when you take the High Road to Taos, a scenic drive that connects Santa Fe to this unique mountain town. The journey itself is as exciting as the destination.

The High Road to Taos is a winding, picturesque route that takes you through beautiful landscapes and small, historic villages. It's about 56 miles long, but you'll want to take your time because there's so much to see along the way. As you leave Santa Fe, the road quickly leads you into the foothills of the Sangre de Cristo Mountains. The landscape changes dramatically, from the high desert to lush forests, giving you a sense of the diverse environment of northern New Mexico.

One of the highlights of the High Road to Taos is the small village of Chimayo. It's known for its history and cultural significance, especially the Santuario de Chimayo, a Roman Catholic church that draws thousands of visitors each year. The church is believed to have healing powers, and people come from all over to pray and take home the sacred dirt that's thought to have miraculous properties. The town also has small artisan shops where you can find local crafts, textiles, and pottery, adding to the charm of the area.

As you continue along the High Road, you'll pass through other picturesque towns like Truchas and Cordova. Each village is steeped in history, and many have been home to artists and craftspeople for decades. The views along the way are breathtaking, with towering mountains in the distance and expansive valleys filled with wildflowers in the spring and summer. The drive can be particularly stunning in the fall, when the aspens turn golden and the landscape is bathed in vibrant colors.

Eventually, the High Road leads you to Taos, a town that has a magical feel to it. Taos is famous for its Pueblo, a historic adobe structure that has been continuously inhabited for over 1,000 years. The Taos Pueblo is a UNESCO World Heritage site, and visiting it is a must to get a sense of the deep Native American roots of the area. The Pueblo's traditional adobe buildings and narrow alleyways offer a glimpse into the past, and the local community is welcoming to visitors who are interested in learning about their heritage.

Beyond the Pueblo, Taos is known for its thriving arts community. The town has attracted artists for generations, drawn by the stunning landscapes and unique light that seems to glow over the valley. You'll find numerous galleries showcasing everything from Native American art to contemporary pieces, and the town is home to the Taos Art Museum and the Harwood Museum of Art, both of which are worth a visit for anyone interested in the local creative scene.

For outdoor enthusiasts, Taos offers a variety of activities. In the winter, the Taos Ski Valley is one of the best places to go skiing in the region, with slopes for all levels of skiers and snowboarders. During the warmer months, you can explore hiking trails, go rafting on the Rio Grande, or simply enjoy the beauty of the surrounding mountains. The town is also known for its hot springs, and after a long day of exploring, there's nothing like soaking in the natural waters to relax.

Taos is also a place of culture and history, with several festivals and events throughout the year that celebrate everything from music to Native American traditions. The Taos Winter Wine Festival and the Taos Pueblo Feast Day are just a couple of examples of the lively events that take place throughout the year.

In all, Taos and the High Road to Taos offer an unforgettable experience. Whether you're driving through the scenic landscapes, exploring the town's rich history, or soaking up the vibrant arts scene, there's something for everyone. The journey to Taos is part of the adventure, and once you arrive, you'll find a welcoming, peaceful town that's full of surprises. It's a destination that will make you feel connected to the land, the culture, and the people of northern New Mexico.

Chimayo: A Spiritual and Artistic Getaway

Chimayo is a small, picturesque town nestled in the foothills of the Sangre de Cristo Mountains, about 30 miles north of Santa Fe. Known for its deep spiritual roots and artistic community, Chimayo offers a unique blend of history, culture, and natural beauty that makes it a must-visit destination in northern New Mexico.

The town's most famous site is the Santuario de Chimayo, a historic Catholic church that attracts thousands of visitors each year. This church, dating back to 1816, is considered one of the holiest places in the region. People come from all over the world to visit the Santuario and experience its spiritual energy. The church is famous for its "holy dirt," which is believed to have healing powers. Visitors often take a small amount of this dirt with them, as it's said to bring blessings or even cure ailments. Whether you're religious or simply looking for a peaceful, reflective place, the Santuario provides a serene atmosphere that invites quiet contemplation.

Walking around the Santuario, you'll notice the beautiful adobe architecture, with its curved lines and earth-toned colors blending seamlessly into the surrounding landscape.

The church is surrounded by small gardens, and the views of the distant mountains create a tranquil backdrop. It's easy to spend time here, soaking in the peaceful energy of the place, perhaps sitting in the garden or walking around the grounds.

Beyond the church, Chimayo is also known for its vibrant arts scene. The town has long been home to local artists and craftspeople, many of whom draw inspiration from the surrounding landscape and its rich cultural heritage. In the heart of the village, you'll find a number of galleries and shops showcasing handmade pottery, jewelry, textiles, and other art forms. Chimayo is particularly known for its weaving, with many artisans creating traditional woven blankets and rugs using techniques passed down through generations. It's a great place to pick up a unique souvenir or gift, and many of the artists are happy to share the stories behind their work.

Another interesting stop in Chimayo is the El Santuario gift shop, where you can find religious and spiritual items, including candles, rosaries, and other keepsakes. The shop's cozy atmosphere and collection of meaningful items make it a lovely place to explore after your visit to the Santuario.

For those who enjoy outdoor activities, Chimayo's surrounding landscape offers plenty of opportunities for exploration. The area is home to hiking trails that wind through rolling hills and scenic vistas. The nearby Chimayo Hills provide a stunning backdrop for a leisurely walk or a more challenging hike. The town itself sits at an elevation of about 6,000 feet, so the views of the surrounding mountains are breathtaking. Whether you're a photographer, nature lover, or simply someone looking to enjoy the outdoors, Chimayo's natural beauty is sure to impress.

If you're interested in experiencing the local culture, Chimayo is also home to a few annual events and festivals. One of the most popular is the Chimayo Ristra Festival, which celebrates the town's agricultural traditions and the iconic red chile ristras that hang from many homes and businesses in the area. The festival features music, food, and a celebration of Chimayo's unique history and culture.

Chimayo is also a great place to enjoy some local New Mexican cuisine. There are a few small restaurants in the area where you can sample traditional dishes like enchiladas, tamales, and chile stews. The food here is flavorful and often made with locally sourced ingredients, including the famous Chimayo red chile, which is known for its rich, earthy flavor. A visit to Chimayo wouldn't be complete without trying some of the local chile, either in a dish or as a souvenir to take home.

Whether you come for the spiritual experience, the art, or the natural beauty, Chimayo offers a peaceful and enriching getaway. The town's blend of history, culture, and stunning landscapes makes it a place where you can relax, reflect, and connect with the heart of New Mexico. It's a perfect stop for anyone traveling through the area, offering a quiet escape with a little something for everyone.

Los Alamos and the Bradbury Science Museum

Los Alamos is a small, intriguing town located about 35 miles northwest of Santa Fe, nestled in the Jemez Mountains. Though it's known for its scientific and historical significance, Los Alamos also offers visitors a chance to explore the natural beauty and peaceful atmosphere of northern New Mexico. The town is perhaps most famous for its role in the development of the atomic bomb during the Manhattan Project, which took place during World War II. But beyond its scientific history, Los Alamos is a lovely place to visit for those interested in science, history, and nature.

A visit to Los Alamos wouldn't be complete without stopping at the Bradbury Science Museum. Located in the heart of the town, this museum is a must-see for anyone curious about the science and history that shaped Los Alamos. The museum, named after J. Robert Oppenheimer, the scientific director of the Manhattan Project, offers a fascinating look into the town's pivotal role in atomic research and its continued importance in scientific advancements.

Inside the Bradbury Science Museum, you'll find a variety of exhibits that explore the history of Los Alamos National Laboratory, the birthplace of the atomic bomb. The exhibits cover a wide range of topics, from the development of the bomb to the scientific breakthroughs that continue to emerge from the lab today. The museum does an excellent job of explaining the complex science in a way that's accessible to visitors of all ages and backgrounds. Whether you're a history buff, a science enthusiast, or just someone curious about Los

Alamos' unique place in history, you'll find plenty to engage with here.

One of the most impressive parts of the museum is its interactive exhibits. Visitors can learn about the science of nuclear energy, the history of the atomic bomb, and the advancements in technology and physics that continue to come from Los Alamos National Laboratory. There are also displays about the people behind these discoveries, including scientists, engineers, and other key figures who contributed to the success of the Manhattan Project and the lab's ongoing research. The museum's hands-on exhibits allow you to get a feel for the science in a fun and engaging way, with models and simulations that help explain how the complex scientific processes work.

Aside from the history of the Manhattan Project, the museum also delves into the more recent developments in science and technology that have emerged from Los Alamos. Topics like supercomputing, cybersecurity, and advanced physics are all explored in the museum, showing how Los Alamos remains at the forefront of scientific research today. Visitors can also learn about the lab's role in environmental conservation and other global scientific initiatives, showcasing how Los Alamos contributes to addressing some of the world's most pressing challenges.

For those interested in the history and natural beauty of the area, Los Alamos also offers many opportunities to explore the outdoors. The town is surrounded by breathtaking scenery, including forests, canyons, and mesas, which make it a great destination for hiking and nature walks. There are several trails that start right in town, offering beautiful views of the surrounding landscape. Whether you're interested in a leisurely stroll or a more challenging hike, you'll find plenty of options to enjoy the natural beauty of the area.

Los Alamos is also home to several parks and green spaces, making it a great spot for a picnic or a relaxing afternoon. One of the most popular parks is Ashley Pond Park, which is located right in the town center. This park is perfect for a peaceful walk or a quiet place to sit and enjoy the surroundings. It's a great spot to unwind after a visit to the museum or to take a break from exploring the town.

When you're ready to explore more of the town, Los Alamos has a small but charming downtown area with local shops, cafes, and restaurants. You'll find a variety of dining options, from casual eateries to more upscale options, serving up everything from traditional New Mexican cuisine to classic American dishes. Many of the local restaurants use locally sourced ingredients, and it's easy to find a meal that suits your taste and budget.

Whether you're interested in science, history, or simply exploring the beauty of northern New Mexico, Los Alamos offers something for everyone. The Bradbury Science Museum provides an in-depth look at the fascinating history of the town and the scientific achievements that continue to shape the world. It's an educational and engaging experience for visitors of all ages. After your visit to the museum, be sure to take some time to enjoy the natural beauty of the area, whether by hiking in the surrounding mountains or simply relaxing in one of the town's lovely parks. Los Alamos is a town with a rich history and a bright future, making it a great place to visit while traveling through New Mexico.

Pecos National Historical Park

Pecos National Historical Park is a special place that offers a unique glimpse into the history of New Mexico. Located about 25 miles southeast of Santa Fe, this park combines the beauty of nature with the rich history of Native American culture and early Spanish settlers. It's a peaceful spot that invites visitors to explore the remnants of ancient dwellings and to walk in the footsteps of those who lived here long ago.

As you enter the park, you'll immediately notice the wide, open spaces with stunning views of the surrounding mountains and the rolling hills. The area is home to the ruins of Pecos Pueblo, a large Native American community that thrived in the area for centuries before Spanish settlers arrived in the 16th century. The park preserves the remains of the pueblo, where you can see the foundation walls of the homes and other structures that once made up the village. Walking among the ruins, you can imagine what life must have been like for the people who lived here, with their community built around farming, trading, and spiritual practices.

One of the highlights of Pecos National Historical Park is the opportunity to learn about the culture and history of the Pecos people. You can visit the remains of the pueblo, which was once home to hundreds of people, and see the place where they lived, worked, and held ceremonies. The site is rich with history, and you'll find informational signs throughout the park that explain what each area was used for. One of the most fascinating parts of the park is the kiva, an underground ceremonial chamber where the Pecos people gathered for religious and social events. The kiva remains in remarkably good condition, and seeing it up close gives you a sense of the deep spiritual connection the Pecos people had to this land.

In addition to the ruins, the park also offers a glimpse into the history of Spanish colonization in the area. In the early 1600s, the Spanish came to the Pecos Valley, and the park includes the site of an old Spanish mission church that was built on top of the ruins of the original Pueblo structures. The mission church was part of the efforts to convert the Native American population to Christianity, and today you can still see the outlines of the church walls and the altar where early settlers once worshipped.

The park is also home to beautiful hiking trails that allow visitors to explore the natural beauty of the area. The landscape is dotted with desert plants, wildflowers, and the occasional glimpse of wildlife. The hiking trails are easy to follow, and the views along the way are simply stunning. One of the most popular trails is the Pueblo Ruins Trail, which takes you through the heart of the ruins and offers views of the surrounding landscape. It's a relatively short hike, making it perfect for those who want to take in the sights without committing to a long trek.

For those interested in learning more, the park's visitor center is a great place to start. The center has exhibits that explain the history of the Pecos people, the Spanish colonization, and the ongoing preservation efforts to protect the park's historical sites. You'll also find a small gift shop where you can pick up souvenirs to remember your visit.

Visiting Pecos National Historical Park is an enriching experience, allowing you to step back in time and connect with the history of New Mexico. The park is relatively quiet, making it a peaceful place to reflect on the past while enjoying the beauty of the surrounding landscape. Whether you're a history enthusiast, a nature lover, or just someone looking to learn more about the Native American and Spanish history of the region, Pecos National Historical Park offers something for everyone. It's a place where you can walk in the footsteps of those who came before, and gain a deeper understanding of the rich and complex history that has shaped this part of the world.

CHAPTER 10.
PRACTICAL INFORMATION

Safety and Health Considerations

Santa Fe is a stunning destination filled with rich cultural history, beautiful landscapes, and unique outdoor adventures. Whether you're hiking through the foothills of the Sangre de Cristo Mountains or enjoying the vibrant art scene in the heart of the city, it's important to stay safe and take care of your health. Here's a guide to keeping safe and healthy during your trip to this enchanting city.

General Safety Tips
Santa Fe is generally a safe city for travelers, but like any popular destination, it's always best to stay alert and take precautions. Be aware of your surroundings, especially in areas with a lot of foot traffic, like the Plaza or Canyon Road. It's always wise to keep your belongings close, especially in crowded places, to avoid pickpocketing. Also, although Santa Fe is known for its charm and warmth, be cautious when venturing into unfamiliar areas after dark. If you're unsure about which neighborhoods to avoid, ask locals or check with your hotel staff for recommendations.

Respect local customs and traditions. Santa Fe is home to several Native American communities, and visitors are encouraged to be mindful of cultural practices and religious observances. Always ask permission before taking photos in cultural or sacred places, and be respectful of local events and ceremonies.

Outdoor Safety

Santa Fe offers an abundance of outdoor activities, from hiking and skiing to rock climbing and mountain biking. While exploring these activities, it's essential to keep safety in mind. If you're planning to hike in the area, start by checking the weather forecast. The high desert climate can be unpredictable, and it's important to avoid trails during storms or high winds. Trails in areas like Bandelier National Monument or the Santa Fe National Forest can be rugged, so always bring a map or trail guide. Pay attention to trail markers, as they'll help keep you on track and ensure you don't wander off the beaten path.

Altitude sickness can be a concern, especially if you're coming from a lower elevation. Santa Fe sits at an elevation of 7,199 feet, and you may start feeling the effects of the altitude, such as dizziness or shortness of breath. If you start to feel these symptoms, it's important to take breaks, drink plenty of water, and rest before continuing your activity. If you're planning to ski or engage in higher-altitude activities, take time to acclimate and avoid overexerting yourself.

If you're going skiing or snowboarding in places like Ski Santa Fe, make sure you're wearing appropriate gear and have a good understanding of your skill level. Ski areas often have slopes for all experience levels, but it's best to start on easier runs if you're a beginner. Always follow posted rules and stay within the designated areas.

Health Precautions

Santa Fe's high desert climate means it's essential to stay hydrated while you're exploring, especially when hiking or engaging in outdoor activities. Carry a water bottle and drink regularly, even if you don't feel thirsty. The dry air can quickly lead to dehydration. Also, since Santa Fe experiences strong sun, even in cooler months, wearing sunscreen is a must. Make sure to apply it before heading out for the day and reapply if you're outdoors for extended periods. Sunglasses and a hat can help protect you from the sun's rays as well.

Because the weather can change quickly, especially in the mountains, dressing in layers is crucial. Start with moisture-wicking clothes to keep you dry, add a warm layer, and bring a waterproof jacket in case of rain or snow. Don't forget to pack sturdy, comfortable shoes if you're planning on hiking or walking around town.

While no specific vaccinations are required for travel to Santa Fe, it's always a good idea to check with your healthcare provider before your trip to make sure you're up to date on general vaccines like the flu shot, tetanus, and any other relevant travel vaccines.

Emergency Contacts
Although Santa Fe is a relatively safe destination, it's important to know where to go in case of an emergency. Below are key emergency contacts:

- Santa Fe Police Department: 505-428-3710
- Santa Fe Fire Department: 505-955-3111
- Santa Fe County Sheriff: 505-986-2480

- Christus St. Vincent Regional Medical Center: 505-984-8000 (For medical emergencies)
- Santa Fe Emergency Medical Services: 505-955-2300
- For outdoor emergencies, such as rescue operations, you can contact the New Mexico Search and Rescue Team: 505-827-9329.

Travel Insurance
When traveling to Santa Fe, it's highly recommended to obtain travel insurance. Look for a policy that covers health issues, medical expenses, and emergency evacuations. These types of insurance are essential in case of accidents, unexpected illnesses, or the need for medical treatment. In the case of outdoor activities like skiing, hiking, or rafting, insurance that includes adventure sports coverage is beneficial. Always read the fine print to make sure your policy covers these types of risks.

Local Health Services
Santa Fe has a number of pharmacies, medical clinics, and urgent care centers to help you should you need medical attention during your trip. Besides Christus St. Vincent Regional Medical Center, there are several urgent care clinics, including:

- Christus St. Vincent Urgent Care: 505-955-3900
- Santa Fe Urgent Care: 505-303-0533

For non-emergency medical needs, pharmacies such as Walgreens and CVS are available in the area, and there are several local health clinics if you need basic care or prescriptions filled.

Resources and Tools
To stay informed and safe, consider downloading apps such as the "Santa Fe Travel Guide" for local events, attractions, and dining recommendations. Apps like "Waze" for real-time traffic updates or "AllTrails" for finding the best hiking routes will be useful. Also, make sure to check local websites for weather updates and trail conditions, especially if you plan to visit areas with unpredictable weather.

Santa Fe offers a beautiful and rich experience, and with the proper planning and precautions, you can have a safe and enjoyable trip. Always remember to respect the environment and local customs, stay aware of your surroundings, and take steps to protect your health during your visit. With these tips in mind, you're ready to explore this captivating destination with confidence.

Local Etiquette and Cultural Sensitivity

When visiting Santa Fe, it's important to be aware of the local etiquette and cultural sensitivities to ensure a respectful and enjoyable experience. Santa Fe is a city rich in history, with a unique blend of Native American, Hispanic, and Anglo cultures. Understanding the cultural norms and being mindful of local customs will not only make your trip more meaningful but will also help you connect with the community in a respectful way.

One of the first things to keep in mind is that Santa Fe is a city that holds its traditions and cultural heritage in high regard. Many visitors come here to explore the history of the Native American tribes, especially the Pueblo peoples, as well as the Spanish influence that shaped the region. Respect for local customs and traditions is essential. For instance, if you visit a Pueblo or any Native American site, always ask permission before taking photos. Many sacred areas and ceremonies are private, and it's important to show respect by not intruding or photographing without consent. Be sure to listen and learn from the locals when it comes to cultural practices. If you're unsure about something, it's perfectly okay to ask questions, but always in a way that shows respect for the tradition or custom.

When it comes to greeting people, a warm and friendly "hello" or "good morning" is the norm. Santa Feans tend to be kind and open to visitors, but it's important to show politeness in conversations, especially when interacting with locals. Keep in mind that Santa Fe has a diverse population, and people value being addressed respectfully. Using terms such as "sir" or "ma'am" can show politeness, but be mindful of not sounding overly formal unless the situation calls for it.

As you walk around Santa Fe, you'll notice that it's a walking city, and many people enjoy the open air of the plaza or the bustling markets. If you're shopping at one of the local markets or galleries, it's customary to ask permission before touching any goods, especially if they are handcrafted items. Santa Fe has a vibrant arts scene, and the local artisans take great pride in their work. When buying from local artists or vendors, always be respectful and take time to ask about the process behind the craft. The artists will appreciate your genuine interest and respect for their craft.

Dining in Santa Fe is an experience of its own, but it's also essential to understand some dining etiquette. Many restaurants, especially those serving traditional New Mexican food, take pride in their regional cuisine. It's common to greet the servers with a friendly smile and thank them for their service. When dining in more casual or family-oriented places, the atmosphere is usually relaxed. But in finer dining establishments, it's expected that you dress neatly and refrain from loud conversations. Tipping is customary in Santa Fe, typically around 15-20% depending on the level of service. If you're unsure about the proper etiquette, don't hesitate to ask the locals for advice.

Another important aspect of cultural sensitivity in Santa Fe is the environment. The region is located in the high desert, and water is a precious resource. It's important to be mindful of the environment and conservation efforts. Many locals are proud of their natural surroundings, and it's appreciated when visitors show respect by reducing waste, recycling, and using water wisely.

Santa Fe is also a place of spirituality and reflection, with many visitors coming to experience its historic churches and sacred sites. The Loretto Chapel, for example, is known for its miraculous staircase and is a place of quiet contemplation. When visiting religious sites, remember that these spaces are often places of worship, and you should behave accordingly—keep noise to a minimum, dress modestly, and avoid disruptive behavior.

Lastly, Santa Fe has a rich blend of festivals, ceremonies, and local celebrations throughout the year. If you're lucky enough to experience one of these events, whether it's a Native American dance, a religious celebration, or the annual Spanish Market, it's important to show respect for the participants and the cultural significance of the event. These occasions are meant to honor traditions and heritage, and your presence should reflect an appreciation for the cultural history they represent.

In short, when visiting Santa Fe, taking the time to understand and respect the local customs can make your visit much more rewarding. Show politeness, be aware of your surroundings, and engage with the local culture in a thoughtful way. Santa Fe is a place that thrives on its rich history, and by following the simple etiquette and cultural norms, you'll be able to have a deeper, more respectful connection to this beautiful city.

Money matters and Currency Exchange

When planning a trip to Santa Fe, one of the first things you'll need to consider is money matters, from currency exchange to budgeting. Santa Fe, like the rest of the United States, uses the U.S. dollar ($), so travelers arriving from countries with different currencies will need to exchange their money.

For visitors coming from abroad, it's important to note that Santa Fe does not use the Euro (€), unlike European destinations. If you're traveling from a country that uses the Euro, you'll need to exchange it for U.S. dollars. The U.S. dollar is the currency widely accepted throughout Santa Fe, and it's used in all aspects of daily life, from restaurants to shops to transportation.

Currency exchange is relatively easy in Santa Fe, but it's best to plan ahead. You can exchange your money at banks or currency exchange offices, but these services typically charge a fee, which can vary depending on where you go. If you exchange money at the airport or in tourist-heavy areas, you might encounter higher fees or less favorable exchange rates. ATMs are another popular option, but keep in mind that many U.S. banks charge international withdrawal fees, so it's a good idea to check with your bank about potential charges before using your card abroad.

To avoid unnecessary fees, I recommend withdrawing cash from ATMs that are affiliated with your bank or use services like those provided by major networks such as Cirrus or Plus. Many visitors also use local exchange offices for cash exchanges, and while the rates are often better than at the airport, it's wise to shop around a bit to find the best deal.

When it comes to budgeting for your trip, Santa Fe offers a wide range of options to suit different budgets. For budget travelers, you can expect to spend anywhere from $50 to $100 per day, depending on your accommodation choices and activities. Hostels or budget motels will cost around $50 to $80 per night, and simple meals like burritos or casual Mexican food can cost as little as $5 to $10. For mid-range travelers, you might be looking at around $150 to $250 per day. This includes staying at a 3-star hotel or a cozy bed and breakfast, dining at more upscale restaurants, and enjoying some local attractions. Luxury travelers can expect to spend $300+ per day, staying in high-end hotels, dining in fine restaurants, and indulging in unique experiences like private tours or spa treatments.

For those visiting Santa Fe, it's good to be aware of some basic costs that will help you plan. Meals can range from inexpensive street food or casual diners for $10 to $20, to fine dining at upscale restaurants where entrees can be $30 or more. Transportation is fairly simple as well, with buses available, but renting a car is often the best way to explore the surrounding areas. Car rentals range from $30 to $70 per day, depending on the type of vehicle.

As for payment methods, credit and debit cards are widely accepted in Santa Fe. Most shops, restaurants, and hotels will take major cards like Visa, MasterCard, and American Express. However, it's always a good idea to carry some cash for smaller shops, markets, or tips. You'll especially need cash if you're shopping at local craft markets, where vendors may prefer it. Mobile payment options like Apple Pay and Google Pay are also increasingly popular, especially at higher-end shops and restaurants.

Another important factor to consider when budgeting in Santa Fe is seasonal pricing. Prices for accommodation and activities can fluctuate significantly depending on when you visit. In the peak summer months, especially around festivals like the Santa Fe Indian Market or the Santa Fe Opera season, prices tend to be higher. If you're flexible with your travel dates, visiting during the off-season (fall or spring) can save you money on both accommodations and activities. Popular tourist spots, like the historic Plaza or the Georgia O'Keeffe Museum, may have higher prices for tickets or services, but local favorites, like tucked-away restaurants or shops away from the main tourist areas, often offer better deals.

One of my own travel experiences in Santa Fe serves as a reminder of how important it is to plan ahead when dealing with currency exchange. On one trip, I made the mistake of changing currency at the airport, where the rates were poor, and the fees were high. As a result, I ended up spending more than I expected. The next time I traveled, I made sure to use a local ATM that had lower fees and better exchange rates, which made a noticeable difference in my budget. Lesson learned: avoid airport exchanges when possible, and take a few minutes to find the best rate.

There are a few great tools to help manage your finances while traveling in Santa Fe. Currency converter apps are useful for checking exchange rates on the go. For budgeting, you can use apps like Mint or YNAB (You Need A Budget) to keep track of your spending. These apps let you set a daily budget, categorize your expenses, and keep your finances in check during your trip.

While budgeting in Santa Fe is relatively simple, being mindful of exchange rates, fees, and seasonal pricing will help you make the most of your trip. Use credit or debit cards for convenience, but always carry some cash for local markets and small businesses. And if you're unsure about the best way to exchange your currency, a little research can go a long way in saving money.

Language and Communication

When visiting Santa Fe, language and communication are important aspects of the experience, especially since English is the primary language spoken. However, understanding a few key phrases in the local language can enhance your trip and help you connect more easily with the people you meet along the way. Santa Fe is a culturally rich city, and while English is widely spoken, you may also encounter influences from Spanish and Indigenous languages, as New Mexico has a strong Spanish and Native American heritage.

Spanish is the second most spoken language in Santa Fe, so learning a few basic phrases in Spanish can be quite useful, particularly when interacting with locals in markets, restaurants, and shops. While Italian and German are not commonly spoken in Santa Fe, you may find some visitors or residents with ties to these cultures, but they are not the primary languages in the region.

To help you navigate conversations and make a positive impression, here are some basic greetings and polite phrases in Spanish. These will be especially helpful in situations like greeting people, making purchases, or asking for directions:

"Hola" (OH-lah) – Hello
"Por favor" (por fah-VOHR) – Please
"Gracias" (GRAH-syahs) – Thank you
"Perdón" (pehr-DON) – Excuse me / Sorry
"¿Cómo está?" (KOH-moh es-TAH?) – How are you?
"Bien, gracias" (BYEN, GRAH-syahs) – Fine, thank you
"¿Dónde está...?" (DON-deh es-TAH...?) – Where is...?
"Cuánto cuesta?" (KWAN-toh KWES-tah?) – How much does it cost?
"Habla usted inglés?" (AH-blah oos-TEHD een-GLEHS?) – Do you speak English?

These are just a few of the most essential phrases you might need when navigating Santa Fe. Having these phrases ready can make interactions feel smoother and more personal, and locals will appreciate your effort to speak their language.

For travelers looking to expand their language skills further, there are many great resources available to help you learn essential phrases before or during your trip. Mobile apps like Duolingo, Babbel, and Google Translate are excellent tools for learning the basics. Duolingo offers lessons that range from beginner to intermediate levels and helps you practice pronunciation through engaging games. Babbel focuses on real conversations, which can be especially useful when you need to communicate with locals. Google Translate can be a lifesaver when you need help translating something on the spot or if you're unsure about a phrase.

In Santa Fe, you'll also find that many people speak English, especially in tourist areas like the historic Plaza, art galleries, museums, and restaurants. Staff at hotels, restaurants, and attractions are generally accustomed to international visitors, so English-speaking assistance is widely available. While Spanish is more common, particularly among the local community, it's not necessary to speak Spanish to get around or enjoy your visit.

As you explore Santa Fe, it's also helpful to be aware of some cultural nuances when it comes to communication. In general, New Mexicans are warm and welcoming, and taking the time to greet people politely can go a long way. A simple "Hola" or "Buenos días" (Good morning) can open the door to friendly conversations. It's also important to be mindful of body language and eye contact. While eye contact is usually appreciated, it's best to avoid staring, as it can be considered rude. A friendly nod or smile works just as well.

Being respectful of the local language and culture is essential in making a positive impression on your trip. Even if you're not fluent in Spanish, trying out a few key phrases will be seen as a gesture of goodwill. It shows that you're interested in learning about the local community and culture, which can help foster stronger connections with the people you meet. Additionally, speaking a few words in Spanish can enrich your experience and help you feel more connected to the vibrant culture of Santa Fe.

Understanding the language basics and communicating with locals, whether in English, Spanish, or a few other phrases, can make your trip to Santa Fe even more enjoyable. As long as you approach interactions with respect, appreciation, and a willingness to learn, you'll find that language is just another way to enrich your travel experience.

Emergency Contacts

When traveling in Santa Fe, it's essential to be prepared for any potential emergencies, whether it's a medical issue, accident, or unexpected event. Santa Fe is a relatively safe destination, but knowing how to handle emergencies and access the appropriate services is important, especially if you're exploring the more remote areas around the city or hiking in the nearby mountains.

Emergency services in Santa Fe are readily available, and the city has a well-organized network of police, fire, and medical services. In urban areas, like downtown Santa Fe, emergency services are quick to respond, with several fire stations, police departments, and hospitals. For rural or remote areas, such as those in the surrounding mountainous regions, services can take longer to reach, but they are equipped to handle situations with the help of specialized teams, including mountain rescue units.

The general emergency number for Santa Fe is 911, which will connect you to police, fire, and medical services. It's a simple number to remember, and the operators speak both English and Spanish, making it easy for travelers from different backgrounds to communicate their needs. If you need to reach specific emergency services, here are the numbers you should have on hand:

- General emergency number: 911
- Local police: Santa Fe Police Department, (505) 955-5000
- Ambulance services: Santa Fe Fire Department, (505) 428-1020
- Fire department: Santa Fe Fire Department, (505) 428-1020
- Mountain rescue services: New Mexico Search and Rescue, (505) 820-1194

In the event of a medical emergency, it's helpful to know where local hospitals and clinics are located. Santa Fe has a few reputable medical centers that provide both emergency and general care. The Christus St. Vincent Regional Medical Center is the city's primary hospital, located at 455 St. Michaels Drive, Santa Fe, NM. They have an emergency department that operates 24/7 and are well-equipped to handle a variety of medical situations. The phone number for the hospital is (505) 820-3000. Another key medical facility in Santa Fe is the Presbyterian Santa Fe Medical Center, located at 4801 Beckner Road, Santa Fe, NM, with an emergency department and general health services. Their contact number is (505) 827-1000.

If you're exploring areas outside the main city, make sure you're aware of clinics and medical services available in surrounding towns. For example, in Española, just north of Santa Fe, the Española Hospital provides emergency care, and you can reach them at (505) 747-6721. Having the contact information for these facilities can be crucial, especially if you're hiking or visiting more remote areas where medical help may not be immediately available.

In an emergency, it's important to remain calm and take the following steps: Dial 911, clearly state the nature of the emergency, provide your exact location, and explain if there are any special circumstances, such as medical conditions or language barriers. If you're in a remote area, giving as many details as possible about landmarks, trails, or nearby towns will help emergency services locate you quickly. Don't hesitate to ask for help in English or Spanish—operators are trained to understand and assist both. If you're unsure of how to speak in Spanish, knowing a few key phrases like "I need help" ("Necesito ayuda") or "It's an emergency" ("Es una emergencia") can be useful.

When traveling, it's highly advisable to have travel insurance that covers medical emergencies, evacuation, and other unforeseen incidents. Many travel insurance companies offer emergency assistance services that can help in cases of serious illness, accidents, or the need for medical evacuation. Be sure to check the specifics of your policy and keep your insurance details handy in case you need them. Some policies even offer a 24-hour hotline where you can get assistance with medical referrals or even transportation to the nearest hospital if needed.

For those planning outdoor activities like hiking, skiing, or climbing, safety is especially important. Always prepare for emergencies by carrying a basic first-aid kit, staying hydrated, and informing someone of your plans before heading out. In remote areas, be sure to check weather conditions before embarking on hikes or other outdoor activities, as the weather can change quickly in the mountains. Recognizing symptoms of altitude sickness, such as dizziness, nausea, or headaches, is also important if you're venturing into higher elevations.

If you ever find yourself in need of help in a more personal way, Santa Fe's residents are generally kind and willing to offer assistance. New Mexicans are known for their hospitality, but it's important to approach them politely, ask for help respectfully, and always express gratitude. Being courteous and acknowledging people's time and assistance will go a long way in building a connection.

Once, during a trip, I found myself unexpectedly in need of medical care after a minor hiking accident in a remote area near Santa Fe. I had no idea where the nearest hospital was, but after calling 911, the operator quickly sent help and got me to the hospital. The staff at Christus St. Vincent were wonderful, and they helped me with everything from paperwork to the medical care I needed. It was a reminder that being prepared with emergency contacts and knowing what to do in these situations is key to handling any unforeseen issues.

For added convenience and peace of mind, there are a variety of emergency apps available that can help travelers stay informed. Apps like Red Cross First Aid or My 911 Emergency Alert can provide valuable tips and allow you to share your location with emergency responders if needed. Checking local websites for updates on weather conditions and possible road closures is also a smart way to stay informed.

While Santa Fe is a generally safe and welcoming place to visit, being prepared for emergencies ensures that you'll be able to handle any situation with confidence. Whether you're exploring the city or venturing into the great outdoors, knowing how to contact emergency services, having the right tools and insurance in place, and being mindful of your surroundings will help you stay safe during your travels.

Useful Websites and Apps

In today's digital age, having the right apps on your phone can make a trip to Santa Fe seamless, enjoyable, and stress-free. Whether you're planning your itinerary, exploring the outdoors, or immersing yourself in the local culture, these apps can be invaluable companions during your journey.

For overall trip planning and navigation, apps like Google Maps are indispensable in Santa Fe. The city's layout is relatively straightforward, but its historic streets and surrounding wilderness areas can sometimes be a challenge to navigate without a reliable map. Google Maps not only helps you find attractions, restaurants, and shops but also provides directions for walking, driving, or public transportation. Pair it with Citymapper, which covers some aspects of public transport, to ensure smooth navigation.

Santa Fe is a haven for outdoor enthusiasts, and apps like AllTrails, Gaia GPS, and ViewRanger are perfect for planning hikes or exploring the nearby mountains and wilderness. AllTrails provides detailed information on popular trails around Santa Fe, including the Dale Ball Trails and Atalaya Mountain Trail, complete with reviews, difficulty ratings, and real-time weather updates. Gaia GPS and ViewRanger are excellent for those venturing into more remote areas, offering offline trail maps and GPS tracking. With these tools, you can ensure safety while enjoying the breathtaking landscapes.

Finding accommodation and dining options is easy with apps like Airbnb, Booking.com, and TripAdvisor. Airbnb offers unique stays that capture Santa Fe's character, from traditional adobe homes to charming casitas. Booking.com simplifies hotel searches, providing filters to match your budget and preferences. Meanwhile, TripAdvisor allows you to explore highly-rated restaurants, many serving local New Mexican cuisine, and even make reservations at top spots like The Shed or Café Pasqual's.

Communicating effectively is crucial, especially if you're interacting with locals or reading signs in Spanish. Google Translate is a must-have, with features like camera translation for menus or signs and offline capabilities if your data connection is limited. For those wanting to pick up a few Spanish phrases before arriving, Duolingo and iTranslate offer simple, interactive lessons.

Safety and emergency preparedness are important no matter where you travel. First Aid by the American Red Cross provides step-by-step instructions for common emergencies and can be a lifesaver in remote areas. GeoSure Travel Safety is another valuable app, offering safety ratings for neighborhoods and real-time alerts to help you stay informed. If you're covered by travel insurance, check if your provider has an app, as many allow you to file claims or access emergency assistance easily.

Santa Fe's rich cultural heritage is a significant draw for visitors, and apps that bring this history to life can greatly enhance your experience. Museum guides like Smartify let you scan art pieces in local galleries, such as the Georgia O'Keeffe Museum, for detailed information. For historical walking tours, apps like VoiceMap provide GPS-guided audio tours that take you through Santa Fe's historic plaza and other iconic sites, sharing stories about the city's unique blend of Native American, Spanish, and Anglo cultures.

Given the mix of urban areas and remote locations in Santa Fe, apps with offline capabilities are essential. Google Maps allows you to download maps for offline use, while apps like AllTrails and Gaia GPS offer offline trail details. Before your trip, ensure you download maps, travel guides, and any important resources to avoid getting stuck without internet access.

To make the most of your apps, ensure your phone is fully charged before heading out each day. Carry a portable power bank, especially if you're using GPS-heavy apps on long hikes. Be mindful of data usage if you're traveling internationally, and consider purchasing a local SIM card or an international data plan to stay connected without incurring high roaming charges.

With these apps and tips, your journey to Santa Fe will be enriched by convenience, safety, and deeper cultural understanding. From navigating the trails to savoring the local cuisine, the right digital tools can make all the difference in creating unforgettable memories in this enchanting city.

CONCLUSION

Santa Fe is more than just a destination; it's a vibrant tapestry of culture, history, and breathtaking landscapes woven together in a way that leaves an indelible mark on every traveler. Its unique charm lies in the harmonious blend of natural beauty and human creativity. The sweeping desert vistas, framed by the Sangre de Cristo Mountains, offer a serene backdrop to the bustling energy of its historic streets. The city's adobe architecture, vibrant art scene, and the mouthwatering aroma of red and green chile infuse every moment with a distinct sense of place. Santa Fe is where outdoor adventure meets cultural immersion, a destination that awakens your senses and stirs your soul.

Reflecting on my own experiences, Santa Fe has always been a place of discovery. I remember wandering through the vibrant stalls of the Santa Fe Farmers' Market, tasting the sweetness of freshly roasted corn and the warmth of locally brewed coffee. Another memory that stands out is hiking the trails in the nearby Pecos Wilderness, where the crisp mountain air carried a silence so profound it seemed almost sacred. These moments reminded me of the beauty in simplicity and the joy of slowing down to truly savor a place.

To fully embrace the Santa Fe experience, step outside your comfort zone. Challenge yourself to hike a trail that takes you to a secluded canyon or summit, rewarding you with a view that feels like it belongs to you alone. Taste something new, whether it's a fiery posole or a decadent slice of blue corn cake, and let the flavors tell you stories of the region's rich culinary heritage. Speak to locals, visit a pueblo, and engage with the traditions that make Santa Fe's cultural fabric so rich. These small but meaningful acts of exploration will make your trip unforgettable.

While the city's iconic attractions, like the Georgia O'Keeffe Museum and the Santa Fe Plaza, are not to be missed, the true magic often lies in the lesser-known corners. Explore the tucked-away galleries of Canyon Road, wander the trails leading to ancient petroglyphs, or venture to nearby towns like Chimayó, where you'll discover a peaceful village famous for its woven textiles and sacred sanctuary. These hidden gems often hold the most unexpected delights and give you a deeper connection to the spirit of the region.

As you travel through Santa Fe, consider the impact you leave behind. Embrace sustainable practices, such as using reusable water bottles, supporting local artisans, and respecting the fragile desert environment. By doing so, you contribute to the preservation of this enchanting place for generations to come.

A few final tips: plan ahead but leave room for spontaneity. Santa Fe thrives on its surprises, from unplanned conversations with local artists to stumbling upon a vibrant festival in the plaza. Engage with locals for their recommendations; they are the true ambassadors of this remarkable city. Above all, allow yourself to be present. Santa Fe isn't just about seeing; it's about feeling, tasting, and immersing yourself fully.

As your journey draws to a close, remember that every traveler brings something unique to Santa Fe and takes something equally unique away. Share your experiences, whether through photos, stories, or simply the fond memories you carry with you. Traveling is as much about the connections you make with people and places as it is about the destinations themselves.

Santa Fe's allure is timeless, a place where past and present coexist in harmony. It invites you to come as you are but promises to leave you changed. Whether it's the beauty of a fiery sunset over the desert, the thrill of an unexpected adventure, or the quiet joy of a shared meal, this city offers something extraordinary to all who visit. Embrace the journey, savor the discoveries, and let Santa Fe inspire a sense of wonder that stays with you long after you leave. It's a place that leaves footprints on your heart, and the memories you create here will linger like the warmth of the New Mexico sun.

MAP

Scan QR Code with device to view map for easy navigation

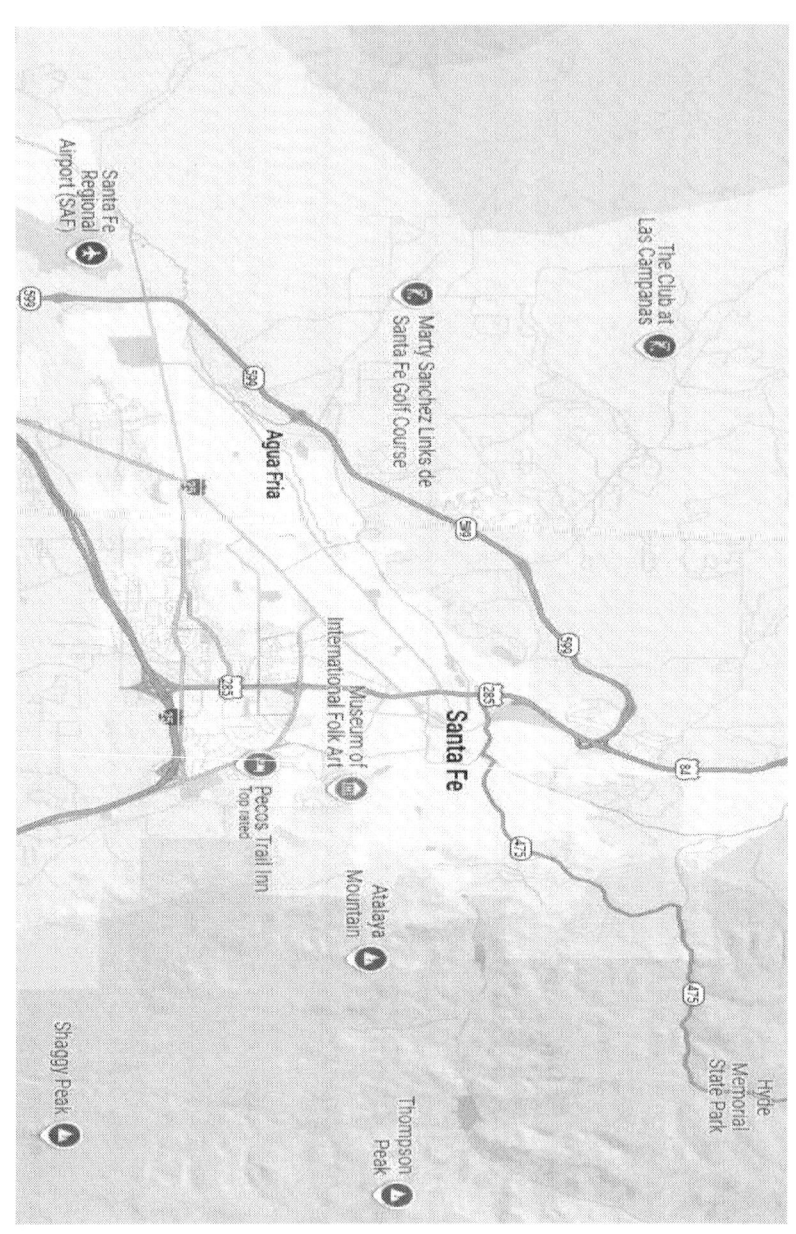

NOTES

Date:

NOTES

Date:

NOTES

NOTES

Date:

NOTES

Made in United States
Troutdale, OR
04/10/2025

30490657R00097